Fraser Harrison was born in 1944 at Stackpole, near Pembroke, and educated at Shrewsbury and Trinity Hall, Cambridge. He then worked for a number of publishing houses, including Sidgwick & Jackson, where he was the editor for five years. In 1975, he left London to live in Stowlangtoft, Suffolk, and write. His first book was an anthology of *The Yellow Book*, which was followed by *The Dark Angel*, a study of Victorian sexuality. In 1982, he published *Strange Land*, his first book about the countryside. Last year he published *A Father's Diary*, and is now working on a further book concerned with childhood, as well as a novel. He has also published short stories and reviews, and is a director of the conservationist group Common Ground. He now lives with his wife and two children in Bardwell, the parish next to Stowlangtoft.

Fraser Harrison

———————————————

THE LIVING LANDSCAPE

Illustrated by Harriet Dell

Pluto Press

London   Sydney   Dover New Hampshire

First published in 1986 by Pluto Press Limited,
The Works, 105a Torriano Avenue, London NW5 2RX
and Pluto Press Australia Limited, PO Box 199, Leichhardt,
New South Wales 2040, Australia. Also Pluto Press,
51 Washington Street, Dover, New Hampshire 03820 USA

7   6   5   4   3   2   1

90   89   88   87   86

Phototypeset by AKM Associates (UK) Ltd
Ajmal House, Hayes Road, Southall, London
Printed in Great Britain by Guernsey Press Co. Limited,
Guernsey, C.I.
British Library Cataloguing in Publication Data available

ISBN 0 7453 0114 2

CONTENTS

To Sal, with more love,
and to our great friends, Marion and Dave Sherwood

ACKNOWLEDGEMENTS

The Chapter 'Who Owns Nature?' is a slightly expanded version of a talk given at the ICA as part of a series of discussions to launch Common Ground. I would like to pay tribute to Susan Clifford and Angela King, the organizers of Common Ground, for their splendid efforts on behalf of conservation, and for providing a medium by which writers and painters can link their work more closely to the conservation movement. My old friend Peter Fuller shares my affection for Suffolk churches and the parish of Stowlangtoft, and I would like to thank him for his stimulating company. Finally, I would like to thank Pete Ayrton of Pluto Press for commissioning the book in the first place, and for his patience throughout its gestation.

INTRODUCTION

As everybody knows, our national heritage of nature is steadily being diminished. From a writer's point of view, one of the worst side-effects of this tragedy is that any description of the countryside is bound to be an exercise in either anger or sadness. No other tone is appropriate. Anyone who writes in a rapturous, or even mildly genial tone lays himself open to accusations of levity, if not nostalgia. The tradition of observing and celebrating the countryside for the benefit of a largely urban readership, which began with Richard Jefferies and reached its peak in quantity, though not always in quality, during the 1930s and 1940s, has given way to a new and much thinner genre, that of conservation writing. This is not the result of dwindling creativity among writers; it is a necessity forced on them by circumstance. When a town is under siege and its buildings are being pounded to rubble by the enemy's guns, it is impossible to shut the door, muffle the ears and sit down to extol the beauties of the architecture that still stands. By the same token, no writer today can blithely pipe songs of pastoral joy while the plough hisses through virgin meadows and the power-saw snarls over its woodland prey. He has no choice but to rage and protest, to wail and mourn, to abuse the villains and weep for the victims. For this is what has become of the countryside: it is now an issue, and no longer a source of amusement and consolation. But by silencing the old music which spoke of a carefree enjoyment of rural nature, modern agribusiness has done far more damage than merely cutting down the expressive range open to country writers; it has also threatened a crucial part of our national sensibility. As much as the innumerable losses to our wildlife, this loss is the tragedy of our time.

In this book, I do not plan to re-examine the ravished limbs of our poor countryside; reports of these outrages are nowadays so frequent they have lost their power to shock. Suffice it to say that according to the Nature Conservancy Council's latest report (1984), 'All main types of ecosystem have suffered appreciable loss [since 1949], but, for some, the scale and rate have been catastrophic.'[1] Although in recent years only one species, the large blue butterfly, has become nationally extinct, this deterioration of habitats and the consequent decline in numbers of flora and fauna has meant that many parts of the countryside have suffered localized extinctions of species that only 40 years ago were commonplace. Despite the efforts of conservationists and the constraints of new laws, the pace of destruction continues to quicken, and the irony is that unless it is immediately slowed (it can, of course, never be reversed) our children will find themselves looking back with nostalgia on our wretchedly depleted countryside, thinking it a very Eden of abundance.

As a writer, one is sure to feel inhibited by the dreadful statistics of ecological loss and the joyless prospect they hold out. But one is also frustrated by the knowledge that ours is a period of insatiable enthusiasm for books about the countryside of the recent past, and especially for books which simply describe its natural history and landscape. There is not a publisher in London who has neglected to discover some long-forgotten writer, exhume his works and trumpet their re-issue under the banner of a 'country classics' series. In the case of Jefferies, W.H. Hudson and Edward Thomas, the giants of this new and ghostly publishing category, every book they ever wrote, regardless of its quality, has or will be reprinted, and every word they ever dashed off for a newspaper is destined to be collected, selected or otherwise anthologized. (Though the literary value of these resurrections is not always certain, we can at least be grateful for a sight of paintings by such artists as George Clausen and other late Victorian rural realists, which make excellent jackets and which have been genuinely neglected.) The appeal of these books surely lies in the fact that they were written before the age of anxiety concerning the environment and its survival. Whatever the motives of their authors at the time, at this second reading they exude in our nostrils an authentic whiff of a countryside whose wildlife was not only enviably prolific, but safe. Even those writers who honourably set out to portray the grim conditions facing the rural poor cannot help but remind us of a vanished landscape which was more beautiful than our own, and they thus become the innocent inspirers of nostalgia.

The queen of such disinterred authors is of course that Edwardian lady with her phenomenal diary. Throughout the summer of 1984, as I was working on this book, her *Country Diary* was making regular entries in the bestseller lists, sales having been reinvigorated by a recent television dramatization and the appearance of a paperback edition. And there were other related books as well, a 'Companion' and a biography of Edith Holden. Not only that, but whole industries were then thriving on the strength of exploiting the iconography – the word is scarcely too grandiose – of the lady's little watercolour sketches. This extraordinary catalogue of achievement is remarkable for any book, but must be a record for a book published seven years previously. It

3

indicates the existence of a great force of feeling in the public, which was released, rather than stimulated, by the Diary; for even its keenest fan would shrink from calling it an inspirational work.

Here, then, is a paradox, which any latter-day country writer must contend with before starting to write: no generation has been more caringly knowledgeable than ours about its countryside and wildlife, or more devoted to its gardens and pets, and yet none has been more relentless in the destruction of its environment. This paradox is not easy to unpick. First of all, hackles no doubt rise at the suggestion that is is 'our generation' which is responsible for decimating British flora and fauna. And rightly so, because it was by no means the general public's fault that British agriculture took the course it did immediately after the Second World War, nor was there much 'we' could do about it once we had learnt how damaging modern farming could be, since the two governing parties were offering effectively the same policies on both agricultural expansion and ecological protection. On the other hand, we cannot be content to wallow in righteous indignation and lay the blame entirely on farmers, or on the agricultural service and food industries. (One must never forget these last two when naming the villains, for they have benefited no less handsomely than landowners from the modernization of farming, and have been as energetic in their lobbying of ministers as the persuasive National Farmers' Union.) If we believe that we, the public, have some rights over the countryside, then we are also bound to take some responsibility for its decline; if we feel strongly that government policy has been misguided, it is up to us, as a democracy, to force the issue on politicians and make it electorally significant.

However, these things are seldom easily or quickly brought about, especially when a more or less ideological and populist movement is struggling to dislodge a deeply entrenched and powerfully connected commercial interest. Though regrettable, it is not surprising that much of the alarm and distress aroused by the news that the countryside is under demolition has been converted into a fascination, an obsession even, for the countryside of the recent past, which to our hungry eye appears to have been ecologically intact.

But whatever one's attitude to these nostalgic longings, there can be no doubt that during the last decade or so our feelings for our countryside and its wildlife have greatly intensified, and the range of their expression has been correspondingly diverse: from the insipid romanticism of television commercials exploiting the notion of 'country goodness' to the near-terrorist activities of certain protection groups, from the compulsion to turn our homes into farmhouses by filling every room with stripped pine furniture to the wildest extremes of eco-freakishness. Apart from buying books or watching television programmes, most people, however, have shown their newly awoken affection for the countryside by simply walking in it, visiting National Trust properties and, above all, by bird-watching, as the astonishing increase in membership of the Royal Society for the Protection of Birds demonstrates.

And yet, despite this outpouring of emotion, there has been very little country writing, and still less landscape or nature painting, of outstanding worth. I use the term 'country writing' with some hesitation, because it suggests a specialism, as in art history, cookery or travel writing, and therefore a limitation, which is neither deserved nor looked for, as it is in these other cases. The countryside is no more specialized a part of our social environment than the town, and the patronizing undertone present in the label 'country writer' becomes audible when it is contrasted with what would be its opposite – 'town writer' – which is absurd and virtually meaningless. To write about the countryside is to write about our common situation; we are all affected, we are all involved. The countryside is not, as is sometimes implied, a remote dependency, a kind of inshore Falkland Islands, whose importance is more symbolic than actual, and whose needs are piously debated, though cynically administered. But, for all that, there is a long-standing tradition of rural literature, largely consisting of writers who have tended to work within the one discipline. And it is the most important branch of this tradition, that of descriptive and observational writing, which has declined recently and has, at best, been upheld by a school of romanticizers, adding short texts to collections of lush photographs.

A review of writers who have made important contribu-tions to rural literature, in its broadest sense, during the last 15 years will perhaps reveal the void I am trying to define. The list below is admittedly arbitrary, being composed of the writers who have had the greatest influence on me, but I hope my point nevertheless remains valid. Nobody interested in the countryside can help but acknowledge a huge debt to Raymond Williams's *The Country and the City* (1973), which for a decade now has been an unfailing source of inspiration, but though it is perhaps his most personal book, it remains essentially a work of literary history. The sociologist Howard Newby is also an academic specialist, who by means of his study of farm labourers, *The Deferential Worker* (1977), has done more than anyone to analyse the reality of social change in rural England since the so-called second agricultural revolution. Using very different methods, John Berger in *Pig Earth* (1979), a sequence of essays, stories and poems, brought together all his powers of imaginative perception to record the impact of change on the peasant community in his adopted French village.

However, despite the remarkable quality of his writing and the fact that he looks on his new neighbours with English eyes, his book has only a tenuous relevance to our rural society, because the phenomenon he is concerned with, the survival of the peasants, is a French, or rather Continental one, which we have not shared since the extinction of our own form of peasantry during the eighteenth century.

Working with their various materials, these writers have enriched our understanding of the modern countryside and, among other things, have helped to establish a much-needed socialist perspective. And yet, though their insights have changed my thinking, they have not broached the vacant space I referred to above. Perhaps the last book to be written in the descriptive tradition was Ronald Blythe's justly celebrated portrait of a Suffolk village, *Akenfield*. In its Penguin edition it is classified under the heading 'sociology and anthropology', which is no doubt correct, but 'topography' would have been almost as apt, for the beauty of the book is that, running through most of the villagers' reported accounts of themselves and their relationships, is an implicit discussion of their relationship with the land and the landscape. Although the book was only published in 1969, it has an old-fashioned air in that it is not overshadowed by an awareness of the ecological crisis, and it belongs, therefore, to another era of 'country writing', quite distinct from the present one. We, on the other hand, belong to an age of grief, which began in the early 1970s, shortly after *Akenfield* was published, when the public first discovered the massive scale of ecological decline. We not only grieve for what we have already lost, but we languish in wretched apprehension of what we will inevitably lose in the future. No writer can honourably ignore these losses, but neither can he shake off the pall of grief. (Since *Akenfield*, Blythe himself has written essays in which he records his sensitive and lifelong affinity with the Suffolk landscape, though as yet he has not written the book this subject demands. The rest of us can only wait with impatience.)

And, finally, there is Richard Mabey, who best exemplifies the point I am making. Of all contributors to conservationism, he has shown himself to be the finest writer: his book, *The Common Ground* (1980), is the most sensitive account I know of both the practice and philosophy of conservation and, more than anyone else, he has insisted on the all-important ethical aspect of the debate. Had the ecological crisis not occurred when it did, he would no doubt have added to the literature of the countryside by writing in the tradition of Richard Jefferies, whose work he has edited. Under the circumstances, however, he has quite rightly allowed the polemical side of his work to dominate. We all have good reason to be grateful for his energy and eloquence, but we must also regret the loss of a writer who might otherwise have commented more extensively on our aesthetic relations with nature, which are problematic enough. On the other hand, perhaps this loss is only temporary; I certainly hope so.

Here, then, is the gap in our country literature. Our knowledge of rural history, sociology and topography has been enormously enlarged during the last 15 years; indeed, I would guess that no previous generation has been as well-informed about the countryside of its day and how it came to be made. Likewise, we are very knowledgeable about our natural history; most people have some understanding of the rudimentary principles of ecology and, thanks chiefly to television, they are familiar with the forms and habits of a large proportion of our wildlife. But, despite this wealth of new knowledge, we no longer know how to respond emotionally and philosophically to nature. We lack an aesthetic which, on the one hand accommodates the awful fact that nature is being killed off, and, on the other, expresses once more our age-old sense of spiritual or imaginative identification with it.

As it happens, no one has felt this need of an appropriate rural aesthetic more keenly than myself. Though born in a remote and decidedly agricultural corner of the country, I have spent most of my life in cities – Liverpool and Shrewsbury, Cambridge and London – and during my early adulthood, when I was living and working in central London, I developed a positive repugnance for the country-side. At that age, confusion and insecurity combined to turn what were, for other people, the attractions of withdrawing to the country into a nightmare for me. On the few occasions when I reluctantly exposed myself to the alleged benefits of rural seclusion and tranquillity, I felt as if I had been condemned to a spell of solitary confinement, with no relief from the miseries of self-reflection. I could find no place for myself in all that mud and greenery; I could get no pleasure from those tracts of vegetable and mineral empti-ness. The clean, refreshing winds did nothing for me except to rattle the frail struts and canvas of my ramshackle personality. To be in the country was to be banished, exiled – in a word, rusticated. Back in the city, I could breathe freely again, having dispersed my self-doubt in the noise and agitation of the street. I enjoyed London for its anonymity, its ceaseless, questing turbulence, its very rootlessness. I was at my happiest just swirling wherever the currents of crowds drove me.

However, here is not the place to describe my recovery from this sorry state, and, in any case, I am not sure I could describe it. Leaving London in 1975 to live here in darkest Suffolk was undoubtedly a vital step in the process, but to this day I do not really know what caused me to move. It is true that my wife hated London and had an affiliation with

East Anglia, so perhaps in reality she made the decision; at all events, my part in it was far more instinctive than rational. Some sound, life-loving drive was at last triumphing over the sterile forces than had hitherto ruled my life.

Initially, my method of adapting to self-banishment was simply to ignore the fact: I sealed myself in my room, concentrated on the work that had brought me there, and seldom glanced outside, at least not with seeing eyes. However, despite my reclusiveness, it was not long before I made the exhilarating discovery that the centre of the universe was not London, as I had previously assumed, but was in fact Stowlangtoft, the village where we lived and where we brought home our first child. Thereafter, my adaptation proceeded smoothly and was soon complete. Even so, it was quite four years before I lifted my head from the desk, stared out of the window and realized for the first time that I had unwittingly made my home in a very beautiful place. This was no doubt a banal conclusion to reach, one that most other people would arrive at by means of a single look, but it filled me with a profound and, at that time, inexpressible emotion.

Aesthetic responses are unpredictable and uneven: for example, not everyone enjoys Mozart at first listening, though to a devoted Mozartian such insensitivity seems impossible in all but the stone deaf. All sorts of cultural and historical factors affect one's aesthetic appreciation, but none will impinge unless one is in a suitable condition of receptivity, and this depends on age, circumstance, experience, emotional maturity and so on. A form or work of art, which once seemed remote and abstract, may suddenly become vividly personal. In art at least, the ears of the deaf and eyes of the blind can be opened; for these disabilities are as much psychological states as accidents of education and preference. Taste is by no means immutable, and at certain stages in life it becomes distinctly volatile. Adolescence is one such stage, and I believe that another is the period of one's so-called prime, when family is well established and work is at its most demanding and fulfilling (or should be in a civilized society). This period is often associated with a new expansiveness in aesthetic taste, as well as a considerable deepening of emotional response. At any rate, so it was for my wife and me. Our move to Stowlangtoft and the birth of our two children had the effect of turning her into a shepherdess and confirming me as a writer (these two activities, both being essentially creative, are not so distant as they may appear). Over the same period, I developed two new passions: one was for classical music, especially the work of those composers who call for a full-blooded emotional involvement – Verdi, Wagner and, above all, Haydn; the other was for the landscape of Stowlangtoft and its immediate vicinity.

I use the term 'landscape' rather than 'countryside' advisedly. During the last few years a great deal has been written, notably by geographers and art historians, on the subject of landscape, its meaning and implications, with the result that the word is no longer easy to invoke innocuously. To designate a piece of land as landscape is, more often than not, to patronize or demean it; for the effect of the label is to reduce the site of other people's lives and work to a mere spectacle. The social reality of those lives does not obtrude on the onlooker, who is left in a happy state of ignorance and indifference. In this way, the connoisseur of landscape endorses and strengthens a set of attitudes which are detrimental to the countryside and the interests of the people who inhabit the landscape, yet are invisible within it. The tourist sees a gorgeous view, but not the lineaments of property, nor the social and political power which property continues to wield; he sees rolling farmland, flush with crops and fat animals, but he does not see that these may be the very forces destroying the view he so admires; he sees the tranquil seclusion of the village, but fails to understand that in reality this is an absence of proper services and public transport. To talk of 'landscape' is, therefore, to run the risk of dissociating oneself from every aspect of the countryside except its aesthetic aspect, and in these days of social and ecological crisis, that is a poor kind of aesthetics.

But, for all that, I persist in applying the term to my immediate surroundings, and I believe I have a perfect right to do so. I do not work on the land, or own any of it, or play any part at all in the processes which shape it. Yet I am not a tourist, and I belong to this patch of countryside as surely as the earthiest farm labourer. I live and work here, and have done so for ten years, which is, incidentally, longer than many other inhabitants, for the populations of our villages are much more mobile than is commonly supposed. I send my children to the local school; I use the local shops and post office; I drink at a local pub and buy my petrol from a local garage. In other words, I am no different from the great majority of my neighbours, who are not farmers either, but earn their living at nearby Bury St Edmunds, Cambridge or Ipswich. But, like the rest of the rural population, we are alienated from our own countryside, because except for the ever-dwindling handful of people who own and work the land, none of us has any control or influence over what happens to our surroundings, and none plays any part in its reshaping. We can only look on helplessly. Whether we like it or not, our agricultural countryside is being converted into 'landscape' – something to look at, but not to touch – and we are being turned into voyeurs.

I differ perhaps in being more closely connected than most to the farming community through my wife, in her capacity as shepherdess. The title may sound absurd, pretentious even, but the reality is not: although her flock is small – 50 ewes in lamb this spring – she is no amateur and the profits from her lambs make up a significant proportion of our income. The group of smallholders to which she belongs are freelance farm workers, small stock keepers and others who work part-time on the margins of agriculture and who now provide a vital link between the general public and the farmyard. In the not so distant past, the farm and its animals were accessible, and it was a commonplace childhood experience to feed the hens, stroke the lambs and let the calves suck your fingers. I have pleasant memories of watching cows being milked on a farm in the suburb of Liverpool where we lived, not four miles from the Liver Buildings. But today animals are not to be found, certainly not to be seen, in the average farmyard and, in any case, children are not encouraged to visit; their parents must turn instead to the smallholder and his back yard.

And so, to return to my emotional awakening, I found myself in possession of strong feelings for the landscape around my home. Inevitably, I wanted to write about my new passion, but was overwhelmed with difficulties; for no sooner had the landscape been revealed as a thing of beauty, than I discovered the countryside to be a tragic problem. In the event, like most other people, I was inspired by the first, but wrote about the second. I could not hit on a suitable mode of expressing my feelings: to rhapsodize seemed indecent, while to bewail the calamity seemed merely self-pitying. Nor, as I have tried to explain, was there any longer a literary tradition to fit into: the writers I admired were either naturalists, who were counting the wildlife that was left, or conservationists, who were counting what was lost. My way through these obstacles at least had the merit of a certain eccentric originality, though it was far from satisfactory. In my book *Strange Land* (1982), I chose to concentrate on the pig, with which my family and I were then on the most intimate terms. I described our ancient companionship with the cottage porker, the jovial pig of medieval iconography, and told the sad story of our estrangement from the modern, factory-fattened beast, and the vile and filthy *pig* of chauvinism and police brutality. I went on to use this divorce as a metaphor of our separation from nature and the agricultural countryside. Thus, I was able to connect theoretical discussions about pastoral mythology and so forth to the flesh-and-blood reality of farming. However, still left out of account were my increasingly intense feelings for nature and the landscape.

I was also very conscious that the gap in the literary tradition corresponded to a dangerous gap in the conservationist argument. Whereas everyone who has written on the subject acknowledges that humanity is spiritually as well as materially impoverished by losses in nature, nobody has yet demonstrated exactly what this human loss amounts to or what its consequences are. This has produced a surprising imbalance: the biological case for conservation has been elaborated to the point where it is indisputable – the only dispute now being how, and at whose expense, rather than whether, it should be put into practice – but the cultural case has not been put at all. Assertion has had to stand in for proof and, despite the tremendous surge of activity on the ecology front, this remains the position.

It is my belief that we, as a species, have an *indispensable* need of an intimate and harmonious relationship with nature, and that if we are deprived of that relationship we will be quite unable to achieve the level of personal and communal wellbeing which is necessary for civilized life. To put it more succinctly, we need nature to make us feel good and to help us make sense of our existence. I would dearly love to be able to parade the anthropological, archaeological and psychological evidence necessary to show that our evolution has made us just as dependent on nature for its symbolism as we are for food, respiration and so on. I would then go on to show, as a matter of scientific certainty, that prolonged divorce from nature and the emptying-out of our age-old symbols will ultimately drive us into collective madness. Unfortunately, however, I lack the training and the ability to co-ordinate these disciplines and I can only hope and wait for the efforts of others.

I also believe that this hole in the conservation case is by no means entirely the result of scientific neglect. It is, to some degree, a moral, rather than an intellectual failing. All of us, not just conservationists, are suffering from a lack of values: we face a moral, no less than an ecological crisis. And because we no longer know what kind of world we should be constructing for the future, we are slow to resist the damage being done in the present, and we turn to past worlds for consolation; because we do not know what we are conserving the countryside for, our campaigns to save it are fraught with confusion and indecision.

However, this book is not going to usher in a new moral dawn, nor is it going to formulate a new aesthetic, much as I would like to see both come about. But there is another kind of testimony, if not evidence, which can be called up to build the human case for conservation, and that is poetic testimony – the description of feeling in response to nature. That, at any rate, is the ambition of this book: to bear witness first to the feelings, and then to the ideas aroused in me by my landscape. If there is to be a new rural aesthetic, it must extend our range of feeling beyond the present alternative of mourning or recrimination. Without indulging in fatuous romanticism, we must achieve a new communion with nature and open an exchange which expresses the full span of our emotions.

It is true that today's wounded and distressed nature is bound to provoke conflicting emotions, as beauty, ugliness and sheer nullity compete to make their different impressions. However, in the end, it is the essential function of conservation to keep the flow of feeling between the human mind and nature running freely, whatever the feeling may be. There is no point in fighting to preserve anything if there is no imagination to respond to it. Come what may, biological life in some form will survive our worst attacks, but the human mind is already showing signs of breaking down – and it is the human mind, therefore, that must be the chief object of conservation.

Finally, a word about the construction of the book: it is divided into more or less self-contained chapters, most of which open with a description of a closely-observed detail drawn from my immediate landscape, and which then expand into a generalized discussion of larger issues relating to our appreciation of today's problematic countryside. The book is therefore somewhat fragmentary, but I hope the reader will discover that each piece contributes to an argument, which though not presented in a linear, step-by-step fashion, nonetheless develops along what might aptly be called organic lines. This introduction is the trunk of the tree, and the chapters are its branches: almost any one limb could be lopped off without killing the plant, but taken together they compose a shape which I have tried to make both coherent and pleasing.

LIVING WITH LANDSCAPE

For the first time in my life I am living in a house with a view; indeed, the word 'view' seems rather inadequate to describe the spectacular prospect this house enjoys.

My family and I recently moved from one end of Stowlangtoft, a small village (population 200) in mid-Suffolk, to the other just beyond, but this tiny shift in distance – we moved no more than a couple of miles – brought about a giant leap in terms of our outlook; for we had risen 50 feet or so, and in Suffolk an elevation of that order is enough to hoist one up to a positive promontory, overlooking huge expanses of countryside.

Our house, which we rent, is built along a line that lies more or less east-west. Behind us, to the north, is 40 acres of woodland, consisting mostly of ash, beech and oak. A straight ride cuts through the trees and gives us from our back door a narrow corridor of view, a true vista in fact, plunging deep into the dark centre of the wood. Apart from this penetrating chink, the trees form a dense curtain, which even in the barest winter months yields only a few feet of its obscurity. But with the backdrop of the wood behind us, looking south, we command an uninterrupted, semi-circular view. Immediately in front of the house, and forever threatening to annex our scrap of lawn, is a large field which dips steeply to a busy lane, also running east-west. Beyond it, rising gently, is a spreading landscape of equally large

17

fields, which are bounded by ditches, the occasional hedge, and a scattering of trees, most of them oaks or moribund elms. To the east, our horizon is fixed by the tops of trees growing along the side of a lane leading to another estate as big as the one on which our house stands. Directly to the south, our view is hemmed in by a ridge standing about a mile away as the crow flies, and running parallel to the one on which our house stands. This too is crested with trees, a copse known as the Stowlangtoft Thicks. Behind them, below our horizon, are the Langham Thicks which run *down* to a piece of ground comically named the Langham Hills. This Lilliputian eminence towers 175 feet above sea level, but its name indicates the significance acquired by the slightest wrinkle or pimple on the surface of Suffolk's flat face. Our most prominent landmark tops the ridge opposite: an enormous cream-coloured water tower, whose vast basin is held high enough to serve even our house. To the south-east there is no hindrance to our view, apart from a cluster of farm buildings a mile away, and we can see, as far as visibility will allow, across the Pakenham fen towards Bury St Edmunds, nine miles beyond. Bury lies below the earth's curve, but on a clear night we can see the lurid glow of its streets lighting up the sky like a sick halo, and during the winter months when the sugar beet is being harvested we can see columns of white smoke rising day and night from its sugar factory. (The factory's short season of activity is impressively referred to as 'the campaign'.) To the west, our horizon is once more confined by trees, though they lie a good distance away and stretch back to the natural horizon, leaving a light charcoal smudge on the sky's lip.

Such is the panorama, or rather the outlines of its canvas, which every daylight hour discloses to the windows of this cottage. No one visits us without commenting on its breadth, the amplitude of our view. In a mountainous

county, or even in a merely hilly one, the square mileage of our view would be small beer, and its lack of dramatic features would make it commonplace. But here in Suffolk, a view is a phenomenon. The irony of a flat topography is that it does not always provide for unimpeded views, but, on the contrary, often allows for the meanest obstacle – a pig shed, a garden wall, even an unfortunately placed bush – to draw a blind over the window. And so, paradoxically, the flatness confines our earthly outlook, pressing us still harder into the mud. But then, at the same time, this flatness inspires an intoxicating sense of release when we lift our eyes and gaze into the enormity of a Suffolk sky. These direct confrontations with heaven's vault perhaps help to explain the fierce religiosity of East Anglia, home of fundamental Puritanism.

Ours is a fat, sleek, rich landscape, a landscape of soft contours and swelling promise, whose fertility has never failed the farmer since he first married his plough to its cleaving earth. It is a thoroughly artificial landscape, and has been since the Romans first drained and paved it, and built their little town, which is about to be buried forever beneath a bypass for the modern village nearby. Its remaining patches of wildness are as carefully maintained as a man's moustache, the last dandyish trace of his primeval hairiness. Nowadays, for the first time in the history of its cultivation, it is inhabited by people who for the most part do not work it or owe their livelihood to it, people for whom the countryside is indeed *landscape* and not a topography of named fields, woods and lanes made familiar – all too drearily familiar – by direct physical contact. Our way of seeing the landscape is much closer to that of the old landowning class than that of their work force: like the squirearchy, we can afford to respond to the countryside as an aesthetic institution, though unlike theirs our view is as powerless as it is profitless.

While I revel in the beauty visible from all our windows, I am also disconcerted by it, for our landscape contains much that would worry the conservationist. The fields we overlook are mostly huge and featureless, the result of a grand programme of amalgamation. Many furlongs of hedgerow have been dug out, leaving only the bare lips of ditches; the fields are empty of trees, which only survive in the few remaining scraps of hedge; there are no farm animals to be seen; and the crops that flourish on these immaculate expanses are disposed in precisely regulated patterns more suggestive of wallpaper than anything organic. And yet, despite this abstract conformation, the combinations of light and moisture that play over the landscape, and the ever-changing tones of brown and green, are always striking, and frequently beautiful.

In fairness, I must add that, unlike certain parts of Suffolk, the modernism of our landscape is relieved by its abundance of trees and copses, which at every turn softens and ornaments the horizon. Furthermore, this estate, which owns our house and all the land around us, while farming its property intensively, is also unusually concerned to compensate for the damage done to wildlife. Trees have been planted along the edges of fields; copses, ponds and other small corners of habitat have been preserved and the wood behind us is sensitively managed. Only last summer the estate dug a new pond, planting it out with a generous endowment of reeds, lilies and so forth, which is designed to act as a flight pond for wild duck and has no commercial use. These are all admirable gestures and they not only throw a lifeline to many locally threatened species, but help to ameliorate the hard profile of a modern farmscape.

As I said, living with a landscape is a new experience for me, and one which has turned out to be deeply pleasurable, though also problematic. To wake up each morning, throw open the curtains and discover a fresh revelation of beauty is exhilarating, but the very fact that the miracle is unfailing day after day, and its range never exhausted, soon prompts one to meditate on the nature of this protean beauty. I have referred to our landscape as if it were a single, constant institution, like an oil painting, but of course that is not the case; nor is it even the case that the landscape has a repertoire of appearances, which it runs through according to the time of the year, state of the weather and so on. No, the truth is that its variety really is infinite. Outside our windows there is not one landscape, there are myriads. The facts of geography may be named and numbered, but landscape is unnameable and unnumberable. Our physical world, despite the onslaughts of modern farming, retains a long enduring consistency; our visual world, however, is merely a fleeting, quicksilver fantasy, a dream, a shadow playing on the cave wall, which dissolves and reforms, evaporates and stands again, approaches, draws back and sometimes slowly drifts, no more than a brown blur behind the hissing rain. The smoke of a morning mist can push the horizon to the very pillars of our porch, but a touch of sun will pierce the veil and show us a landscape so crystal sharp that every leaf seems to have been polished and every filament of spider's web spun from silver. Our visible world is restlessly evanescent; it possesses less stability than a cloud running in shreds before a gale, less solidity than the surface of a brook tugged from below by its current and agitated above by the erratic breeze. Landscape was a mirage I never thought to question, but since coming here I have been disturbed and excited by its hallucinations, its continual bending and stretching, its ceaseless mutation of the physical out-of-doors on which I used so blithely to rely for constancy.

Nor do these changes come about by a gradual or gentle process; as often as not they occur suddenly, only to be replaced just as abruptly. A mere hour can see a whole series of transformations, and when weather, season and modern agriculture combine to alter the land, the result is nothing short of revolutionary. Take, for example, three days in September: in the early morning of the first day the field opposite our house was a tranquil vision of tawny, ripe barley, the wind softly rippling its mane. But already a combine harvester was at work and by evening we could see its lights cutting the half-dark at the bottom of the field as it cropped the last acre. The next day brought Armageddon. We had no chance to take in the new scene because it was being put to the torch. The long straggling drifts of straw left by the harvester took only a single match each to light and by breakfast we were ringed with fire, while the sky above was scorched. The sudden heat was so intense black ash and smoke were hurled directly upwards to form a dense, coiling tower, which only began to fray and disperse a hundred feet up when it was struck by sharper, atmospheric winds. The fierce heat also chucked aloft big lumps of unburnt straw and these fell audibly in the garden and on to our roof like missiles. But by lunchtime the flames were out, the crackling was silenced and there was nothing left of the conflagration apart from a few idle wisps of smoke hovering over the charred weals where the straw had been gathered. The field looked as if it had been scourged by some gigantic flail, but that afternoon the children were still able to make their camps in the heaps of straw that had escaped the fire. On the morning of the third day, we woke to discover a tractor ploughing up the burnt and unburnt stubble and turning yesterday's raw scalds into the smooth voluptuousness of yielding soil.

These changes overtake the countryside with a speed and finality never experienced by the town except in wartime or during major catastrophes, such as floods and earthquakes, which are very rare in Britain. Snow is perhaps the only natural phenomenon that regularly effects a complete transformation of our townscape and landscape alike. For those of us lucky enough to have access to an expansive view, whether rural or urban, it is impossible not to think of the shifting scene beyond the window as theatre. Whatever else it might be, a fine landscape is always a spectacle, and the country resident, whatever else he or she might be, is always something of a spectator. And I insist there is nothing despicable in treating the countryside as an aesthetic object; nor does it show a lack of some indispensable authenticity, without which you are debarred from being a true country person. Whether we like it or not, most country people now occupy the position of spectator in relation to farmland and it is for us, more than anyone else, that a new rural aesthetic is needed. This must provide us with a way of seeing the countryside which admits no sense of inferiority to farmers and is fully alert to the process of destruction, but is not ashamed of its emotional response to sheer scenery.

We have looked at our landscape, our small patch of England's well-fed belly, for nearly a year now, observing all its nuances of mood and appearance. Through this intimate familiarity we have formed a powerful bond with the terrain itself, though of course other forces have been at work too. The space outside the window remains a proscenium, a stage on which the drama of landscape is played out hour by hour, but it has become enriched with other meanings, some literal, some symbolic and some which are much harder to describe and lie close to the heart.

From my childhood in Liverpool I remember a large street plan of the city that used to stand outside Lime Street Station. Dotted all over it were different coloured little light bulbs and below was a panel of buttons labelled 'Cinemas', 'Theatres', 'Railway Stations', 'Hospitals', and so forth.

When you pressed a button a sprinkling of bulbs, all the same colour, would light up showing the whereabouts of these respective places. Blue, I recall, was the colour for cinemas. Apart from having the great virtue of being free to use, this splendid machine gave me many happy moments because it seemed to grant the freedom of the city; its services and entertainments, everything it had to offer, were yours to command at the touch of a button. But I also used to enjoy the idea of reducing the city to its elements: a sudden bloodbath of red-bulbed hospitals, a frenzy of stations, or, best of all, the city converted into a paradise of cinemas and theatres.

By a simple trick of perception, I can produce a similar effect while standing at our window. I press one imaginary button and our network of roads lights up: here is the road that leads to Bury St Edmunds and thence to Cambridge, to bookshops, cigar shops, restaurants and all the ambivalence of spending for need or pleasure; in the other direction, the same road leads to the paddock where Sally keeps her sheep, and beyond to the village where the children's school stands; yet another road leads to the water tower on our nearest horizon and down to the core of Stowlangtoft village. This is our life revealed as a route map. A second button throws an estate agent's plan onto the screen of our window, every property staked out and labelled with its owner's name. A third button reassembles the view into a parish topography, marking the fields, streams, copses and ponds with local names not shown even on the Ordnance Survey. With a fourth button I can turn the land into an agricultural study, with each crop colouring our panorama identified and valued. A fifth gives a gamekeeper's plan, showing the haunts of vermin and predators, the sites of traps, pigeons' feeding grounds, and shared boundaries with rival shoots where pheasants can be lost. And a sixth lights up the geography of our social life.

This is a game, but it serves to illustrate the fact that our perception of land is no more stable than our perception of landscape. At first sight, it seems that land is the solid sand over which the mirage of landscape plays, yet it turns out that land too has its own evanescence. A closely observed, familiar and lived-in topography adds up to a very complex compound of signs and meanings, all of them in a state of perpetual change. Place – if *place* is the word to describe the unity of one's own land and landscape – is a restlessly changeable phenomenon, manifesting itself variously as 'parish', 'home', 'constituency', 'beauty spot', 'school catchment area', or even as 'prison', 'land of exile', 'suburb', 'commuter dormitory', and so on. The place we live in, look at, use, and pay for, will not diminish itself to a simple, fixed title: Stowlangtoft is, for each of us, a separate and unique notion, as much a private symbol as a village.

OUR CONKER TREE

Standing beside our house is a mature horse-chestnut – a conker tree. Round the trunk it measures about 11 feet and, using the rough gauge of an inch for every year of growth, this suggests it was planted sometime in the middle of the last century, perhaps when the house itself was built. It is in the full vigour of its maturity. The crown and upper branches are still throwing out fresh length and we will soon have to lop off a limb which threatens to force its way into our daughter's bedroom. Lower down, the knobs and burrs on its trunk and the exposed thighs of its roots have to be shaved each year to prevent their bristles of new growth from darkening our kitchen. The plates of bark on its trunk are formed in thick, rugged corrugations, whose colours alternate between the vivid green of some lichen and their own purplish brown. These battered folds appear to have been under terrific torsion, as if somebody had once tried to twist off the tree's head and then given up, leaving the buttress bark as contorted as a sheep's horn. Despite its malformed torso and the mass of knotted branches above, none of which extends for longer than six inches without writhing back on itself, the spread of its crown is elegantly spherical and in summer the foliage resembles a buoyant, hovering green balloon secured to the ground by the straining cable of its trunk.

The word conkers may derive from an association with

conquers, but since the game was originally played with conch shells, known colloquially as *conkers*, it more likely derives from the shells as does *conk*, the slang word for nose. The earliest appearance of the word is given by the *Shorter Oxford English Dictionary* as 1877, which makes it younger than our tree. The species, however, has been in the country since the early seventeenth century (1629), when it was introduced as a fashionable border for avenues. Its origins are obscure; at one time it was believed to have been a native of Tibet, carried from there to England as early as the mid-sixteenth century, but now it is thought to be indigenous in the mountains of northern Greece, and 1576 seems to be the date when it found its way via Istanbul to Vienna, whence it rapidly spread throughout Europe. Its name (*Aesculus Hippocastanum*) is supposed to derive from the use of its nuts by the Greeks and Turks as a cure for glanders, coughs and short-windedness in their horses.

In the past, its bark and nuts had a few commercial applications: the nuts were used in making oils, cosmetics, starch, bookbinder's paste and so on; the bark was used in tanning and dyeing and, for a while, it enjoyed a vogue as a tonic. Powder from the dried nuts was at one time prescribed as a kind of medicinal snuff and, mixed with alum water, it was held to be a powerful rat poison. The wood, which is soft and non-durable, was only good for making water-pipes and small, easily-worked objects, such as toys, trays and bowls. Otherwise, it was used as fuel and as a source of charcoal for gunpowder. But it was never planted in mixed woods for profit, since it is greedy for light and space, and tends to overwhelm its neighbours.

In practice, the horse chestnut is almost exclusively ornamental, and is planted for the splendour of its shape, especially when arranged in rows or avenues, and for the exquisite beauty of its flowers – its so-called candles. In this respect it differs from the Sweet Chestnut, to which it is botanically unrelated, because the Sweet Chestnut is not only beautiful but valuable too, having hard wood suitable for building and fence poles.

To be on intimate, almost semi-detached terms with a fully-grown tree is in itself a singular experience, one which I have not had since my childhood when we shared our meagre front garden with a massive, oozing lime. There is something impressive, as well as daunting, about having as an immediate neighbour an animate, though incommunicative being, which stands substantially taller than our roof and occupies as much space as a small house. And it is impossible not to sense a close correspondence between the routine of our family household and the vegetable life of the chestnut. Both house and tree, in their different ways, are institutions, each having its own community, its own terms and seasons, its own traits and peculiarities; and both institutions share the same purpose, that of fostering the growth of the next generation. At no time of the year does the tree appear to be at rest; even now, in late November, its conkers having long since fallen and the last of its rusting leaves having blown off in yesterday's gale, its work goes on as it pumps life into next spring's black buds, which are already well formed and coated in their protective gum. Like a family, it is ceaselessly active. However, unlike the oak, which seems unable to achieve anything without a convulsion of effort, the chestnut attains a profiency that is more industrial than natural. It vibrates with a smooth and continuous productivity, culminating each year in its titanic output of conkers.

Despite looking well-rounded and ready to drop, the conkers refused to surrender to the siege of sticks and rocks waged all summer by my small son and his friends, and it was not until the second week of October, on a brilliantly hot Sunday, that they began to fall in earnest. Friends, who

were taking advantage of this last flash of Indian summer by sitting beneath the tree, were forced to retreat under the bombardment. Throughout that day and night, and the next three days and nights, there was a continual crashing and thudding as the spiny husks tore through the leaves and hit the ground, where they split and discharged their clutch of sleek conkers. And even after the deluge had slackened another week passed before this prodigious crop was finally unloaded. By the end the tree's marathon spasm had deposited a heap around the base of its trunk as deep as a bed of shingle. I set my children to count this marvel of super-abundance, but the quantity far outdistanced the few hundreds they could manage to keep in sequence. The total certainly ran into thousands.

The beauty of conkers has its own sharp melancholy. As soon as they are exposed to air and light the glossy, mahogany polish that shines in the mottled grain of their rind begins to fade, and within minutes their skins dry to a lustreless mat, which no amount of handling or rubbing will reburnish. The jewel turns into a pebble in front of your eyes. It is possible to find old conkers buried in the grass which have preserved a little of their original glow, but it dims when they are picked up because they are only damp and lack the true shoe-polish sheen of conkers fresh from the waxy clasp of their shells. Nor does the pale patch at the bottom, where they draw life from their husk-wombs, ever keep its first floury whiteness.

Though my great neighbour fascinates me, it disturbs me too. This mighty being lives next to us and resembles us, it is admired by our friends and entertains our children, it shades us from the sun and protects us from the wind. With its globe of summer green, its brief ball of autumn fire and its lobster basket of tangled winter branches, it turns our house into a spectacular landmark. And yet, in spite of its many remarkable qualities, I do not feel at ease with it; in fact, I recoil from the inexorable march of its reproductive cycle.

It may seem absurd to think this way about a mere tree, but I defy anyone to share a home with such a prodigal and restless organism and remain impervious to its presence. We project our feelings onto nature, and nature, in its turn, deeply affects the tone of our emotional life. The weather uplifts or dispirits us; spring revives our hopes, while autumn reminds us of our transience; we see our own domesticity in the house martins' mud huts, and in the poignant call of the cuckoo we also hear the voice of family ingratitude. The great forms and forces of nature – the sea, cliffs, clouds gathered around the setting sun, mountain ranges and so on – seem to be expressive of our most profound emotions, to which we can hardly put names except by associating them with ideas of our ultimate destiny. In short, we feel an affective exchange exists between ourselves and nature.

The cycle of life and death in nature offers the most accessible and emotive representation of our own biological fate. This metaphysical view of nature helps us reconcile ourselves to those aspects of our flesh and blood existence which are least compatible with our self-knowing intelligence. By identifying our feelings and life story with animal behaviour and the rhythms of renewal and decay in plants, we give meaning to the key moments of our existence, and keep up our courage in the face of our mortality and vulnerability to suffering. It is only 'natural' that we should think of these biologically determined episodes – birth, growth, sexual bonding, nurturing, ageing, sickness and death, the mysteries which are the heartland of any religion – in terms of symbolism drawn from the life processes of other organic creatures.

No one except the most stringent and least imaginative

botanist looks at the plant world as purely vegetative, just living out its organic fate. During our evolution as a species we developed an acute responsiveness to the environment, and because we lacked the kind of specialist abilities other animals had refined, our responsiveness was nearly comprehensive, involving all the senses. As omnivores, we could not afford to overlook any potential source of food, wherever and however it grew; as opportunist hunters, we learnt to predict the behaviour of our prey; and, as relative weaklings, more dependent on our wits than our strength or ferocity, we know our topography inside out – where to hide, where to lie in wait, where to gain a clear view of our predators and victims, and where to make camps in which we spent our intensive family life. As the geographer, Jay Appleton, has pointed out, a mere two hundred generations separates us from our Stone Age ancestors, and it is hardly likely that in such a short space of evolutionary time we would have lost their keen sensitivity to the environment, which was for them 'a prerequisite of physical survival'.[1] But this is only half the story, and the least interesting half at that.

Our knowledge of the environment was by no means confined to the practical, for our botany and ethology were indivisible from our religious ideas about plants and creatures. Indeed, the very formation of the human mind was bound up with its animistic perception of the physical world, from which our newly-dawned self-consciousness had only recently put us apart. The annual cycle of plant life, the variety of behaviour and appearance in animals, the vicissitudes of the weather, the motion of the stars and planets, the power and regularity of the sun, the mysterious variability of the moon – all these natural features provided material for the symbolic systems, the mythologies, which primitive humans invented in order to shape their understanding of the world and their place in it. Natural phenomena were translated into myths to explain the way their universe worked.

At this stage in our evolution, religion and science were inextricable: the one did not recede as the other advanced. The retreat of religion in the face of scientific discovery is unique to modern history, to which we have as yet failed to adapt. The practice of magic and the daily business of getting a livelihood were one and the same thing, and it is even thought that religious priorities were probably the driving force behind the accumulation of knowledge, of which the practical application was only later appreciated. Take, for example, the domestication of cattle. Their ancestor is generally agreed to have been the wild urus, a massive and ferocious beast, whose curved horns had magical significance by virtue of their resemblance to the moon's crescent. According to Erich Isaac, the motive for domesticating this redoubtable creature was inspired by the need for a ready supply of mature, but tractable stock for use in ceremonial sacrifices.[2] Once they had been subdued by selective breeding, to say nothing of ritual castration, the docile descendents of the sacrificial urus became obviously more desirable for secular uses. Thus, the religious impulse decisively anticipated the economic. It appears that this was the common pattern and that most advances in civilization during the era of pre-history were connected in origin with a sophistication of religious practice.

The objects of thought on which the human mind nourished itself during the period of its maturation were inevitably drawn from the natural world. Later, the growth of agrarian civilization and then the emergence of cities invested the natural arena with different sorts of significance. In modern times, attitudes to nature have proved very changeable: even over a period as brief as the last four hundred years our ideas have undergone a complete inversion, from the Elizabethan belief, sanctioned by Genesis, that the earth was created solely for Man's benefit and pleasure, to our conflicting beliefs in the need to conquer and conserve nature. However, throughout these phases of attitude, nature has prevailed as the richest source of metaphor with which to illuminate the human condition. Our present-day sensitivity to place and landscape is still made up from that primitive union of opportunism and magic, though for most of us, the business of 'reading' the landscape has resolved into an aesthetic activity. Our survival is no longer dependent on our individual skills and alertness as hunter-gatherers or as farmers; we live in a market economy and, for better or worse, leave these jobs to specialists. However, the potential for that kind of resourcefulness remains a part of our common genetic heritage. We no longer invest the natural world with spiritual life, even if certain kinds of 'holistic' ecology come perilously close to doing so, and the unbelieving majority of us do not regard the wonders of nature as evidence of divine creativity; nature is no longer the handiwork of God, it is its own creation. Yet, for all that, we still retain a 'religious' perception of landscape, that is a capacity for discovering in nature a symbolic representation of our deepest concerns and aspirations.

Without a formal religious language to express our feelings for nature, we run the danger of allowing our responses to collapse into the worst kind of anthropomorphism. Not that all kinds of anthropomorphism are blameworthy; on the contrary, it is an essential part of our imaginative make-up that we perceive in, and project onto the outside, objective world images and likenesses of human experience. How else could we make our way in an arbitrary universe? Our identification with nature is the gift – and curse – of self-consciousness. Every image is at once a celebration of our unique imaginative powers and a dismal reminder of our inescapable fate. No, this identification with nature only becomes sickly when it refuses to see anything except its own shadow, when the tiger no longer burns in the forests of the night, but is made to prance about on the seashore personifying motor oil. Then, of course, nature is denied and our fantasies begin to feed on themselves, growing gross with under-nourishment.

Close proximity with a large virile organism, such as our conker tree, ensures that sentimentality does not colour one's perceptions. Despite the many similarities between the big tree and our household, I am no less aware of its organic life than its poetic suggestiveness. Ironically, this is for entirely poetic reasons: I interpret the chestnut's large, tumescent buds with their sticky tips, its eagerness to show its leaves early in spring and shed them early in autumn, its ravishing flowers and, above all, its prolific outpouring of seed, as signs of an exceptional reproductive drive. Living close to this continual and very conspicuous display of sexual energy makes it impossible not to feel the tree's complete unconcern for human affairs, its unconcern for anything other than the generation of more of itself.

But if the chestnut's throbbing procreation dries up any sentimentality that might be lurking within me, it does not prevent my feeling a strong sense of reciprocation with the landscape at large. In modern times, our English sense of reciprocation with landscape has been badly starved. For most people, contact with nature has now diminished to the point where it is negligible; and, meanwhile, nature itself, by being rooted out to make way for crops and concrete, has also been tragically diminished. Our symbolic perception of the living world, which in differing ways for different generations has for so long helped us to understand our role in existence, is being famished on two sides. This malnutrition has driven many into a frenzy of conservation, while many others have fallen into a nostalgic trance, dreaming of fuller days. But, it has to be acknowledged that a yet greater number of people have, out of expedience, developed new and far less healthy tastes, becoming indifferent to the emotional resources which even a beleaguered nature has to offer.

And yet what I dread still more than an indifferent nation is an indifferent landscape. I fear the continuing expansion of a landscape which cannot reciprocate, which refuses the old interchange of feeling, which forbids the transformation of nature into symbol, and leaves the ravenous imagination nothing to feed on but itself. I fear the coming of a countryside which is so intensively farmed its landscape will be too barren to respond to our emotional needs.

As with all profound aesthetic responses, there is a vigorous element of magic in our perception of landscape: we see what is not there. But I have a nightmarish vision of a landscape drained of magic, inhabited by a population which sees only what *is* there and responds only to nature's shadows transmitted onto screens and traced in books. I foresee a countryside stripped of poetry and supervised by a society which prefers the geometry of agriculture to the wayward tangle on its shrinking margins. I see a countryside impervious to symbolic suggestion and dead even to sentimentality, a blank landscape confronting a blind nation. Then nature will be meaningless, a mere perpetration of animal and vegetable energy, and the chestnut will be nothing but a spike of green tissue, fatuously working out its botanical process.

This is how the light could fade: not eclipsed by the storm-clouds of nuclear winter, nor by the fog of pollution, but put out by the blinding of our imagination. Above all, it is the job and responsibility of conservation to keep alive the landscape's poetic faculty.

WILD FLOWERS

Far from being a merry month, May has turned out this year to be a cheerless extension of winter, a wet, cold, unrelentingly grey fraud of a month. The field in front of our house has been flooded again and again, and its crop of seedling sugar beet has been shredded with bombardments of huge hailstones. From the comfort of our kitchen window we have even watched cars halted by impenetrable snow blizzards in the lane below, an entertainment usually reserved for the Christmas holidays. And so, on one of the few mild and sunny days to occur this month, it was with more than ordinary seasonal high spirits that my children and I walked down the path into the woods behind our house to inspect the wild flowers.

This brief spell of warmth and light seemed to have injected an extra urgency into the behaviour of the birds. The trees that screen our garden rang with the sharp cries of chaffinches, and their quick sorties across our lawn – whirr and glide, whirr and glide, their striped wings and white tails flashing with each spasm of flight – did not stop for us. A pair of robins with young to feed were likewise indifferent to us, concentrating instead, heads to one side, on a patch of bare shrubbery I had toilfully dug over the previous evening. Only a cock pheasant, strutting in idle and solitary pomp now that his hens had chicks to rear, saw us as a threat, and he made a futile, crashing leap into the nettle and bramble undergrowth, squawking with alarm. Once inside the wood, though every tree reverberated with bird song, we could only see the occasional blue tit, as it flitted among the topmost branches, pausing to release a call that seemed impossibly loud for so small an instrument. Our progress along the path was marked, however, by successive volleys of flapping pigeons shooting from their roosts in the crowns of the biggest trees. The children's voices ensured that they fled long before we approached them, but even when I walk here alone my softest footfall is sufficient to alert them a hundred yards away. Each volley wheeled above us in a great scattering grey cloud, which gradually gathered itself in the sky until the birds settled once more in a solid mass to roost in a different tree. The trees themselves are mostly ash and were then still in their winter skeletons, their spreading silhouettes thickened by black buds that would not burst for another two or three weeks. Oaks are the next most numerous and their leaves were showing, though they did not yet conceal their branches, and were only dense enough to give the impression at a distance of a soft green haze, almost a mist, floating around each bare trunk.

Walking through the wood at this time, and on such a day, I could not help but think of Hopkins's line in the poem *Spring*, 'What is all this juice and all this joy?'. Every vegetable fibre was turgid with new sap, every branch was throbbing with generative energy and straining to squeeze out fresh life; the very ground itself heaved with the effort of delivering newborn tissue. And it was impossible not to hear in the chorus of bird song a note of jubilation that was quite unattributable to the mundane business of mating, nesting and feeding; this was singing for its own sake. I defy anyone who has been lucky enough to hear a nightingale sing, as we were during this same May, to explain away that magical, eerie melody entirely in terms of a congenital response to stimuli. Keats was surely right: somewhere in that music there is ecstasy.

As it happened, a few weeks earlier we had been able to stand in our garden and listen to spring actually bursting out, not from a full-throated bird, but from a tree. In front of my study window is a Scots Pine, which is in most respects a handsome specimen, except that it lists at a crazy angle of 45 degrees, and only a massive counterbalancing limb growing parallel to the ground saves it from being uprooted by its own weight. According to local legend, its Pisan lean is the result of a blow struck by a negligent tank on practice manoeuvres during the Second World War. At all events, the tree thrives. Towards the end of April, I was puzzled one warm evening by a crackling noise coming from the direction of our lopsided tree, and, never before having lived at close quarters with a Scots Pine, I had to stand right beneath its branches before I was able to identify the source of these little detonations. The tree's cones, which though in their second year of growth had only recently become hard and woody, were beginning to open, scale by scale, and each of these imperceptible unfurlings was producing an audible 'pop'. Presumably under the combined influence of the season and the mild weather, the process was going at full speed, and the resulting noise was a louder version of the 'snap, crackle and pop' of breakfast cereal fame. Here was spring in the very act, as it were, of being sprung.

At the end of the 100 yard tunnel formed by the trees overhanging the ride that leads from our house into the woods is a large open space of an acre or more, which was created during the winter when part of the wood was coppiced. Here I made my children stop and sit with me on the stump of an ash. They were easily persuaded to do this because it was heavily encrusted with revolting fungus, which was irresistibly suggestive of faeces and therefore the

object of much delighted interest. The recent clearance has exposed large patches of wood floor where sunlight has not shone strongly for many years, and as a result the whole area is rife with wild flowers growing among the spikes and stools of coppiced ash. Dog's mercury, rather than grass or nettles, has invaded to cover the floor with a green carpet, but being quite short and widely spaced it has left room for a great variety of other plants to multiply.

Near our strangely ornamented stump was an irregular-shaped cushion of flowers which were massed together so richly we went to look more closely. The margins of our walk through the wood had been sprinkled with different flowers, but here they were all collected in great profusion on what must have been an especially fertile spot. Most conspicuous, because of the shining purity of their white star-like flowers, were wood anemones. A few were flushed with pink, but all the drooping, unopened buds were tinged purple. In another constellation were the yellow, glossy flowers of lesser celandine, gold to the anemone's pearl. Below both these, and hardly visible beneath their soft hairy leaves, were the small violet flowers of ground ivy. The dog's mercury had already flowered, but its upright catkin spikes of tiny dried-out blooms were still showing. Here and there, poking above the tangle of green, was the odd bugle, its whorls of blue and copper flowers forming a sort of jewelled handle whose blade was buried in the ground. And, above them all, acting as a protective barrier of natural barbed wire, were the prickly coils and loops of bramble, as yet flowerless. The children picked a sample of each flower to keep for pressing, and, not forgetting to break off a piece of their dungy fungus from the wood stump, we returned home.

Now, I would be a fraud if I left the impression that the birds, flowers and trees in our wood were immediately recognizable to me, and that I had a lifelong familiarity with our common flora and fauna to draw on. The truth is, sadly, the contrary. Before we came to live here, my knowledge of natural history was the minimum that might have been expected in an unperceptive city dweller. I could identify most of our native mammals, not on the strength of actual observation, but because they were literary figures. Although I can remember being shown at my preparatory school how to cure a mole skin, something I could still do today if I had to, just as I could still make an instrument for imitating the call of red deer (such are the incalculable advantages of a private education!), I do not remember seeing a live mole until 1975 when we took over the tenancy of an infested lawn along with our first house in Suffolk. Up to then, my notion of the mole had first to be stripped of E.H. Shepherd's yeomanly waistcoat and shirt-sleeves before it conformed with the living creature. This is not whimsy on my part, but simply the product of experience circumscribed by books, for my idea of nature owed more to the bestiary of children's literature than zoology. The badger, water rat, toad, stoat and weasel were discovered in Kenneth Grahame, as was the otter, though more reliably in Henry Williamson as well; I learnt about seals from Kipling, the inner lives of horses from Anna Sewell, and the tribulations of hedgerow animals from Beatrix Potter. Because poetry is not usually illustrated, the celebrated birds of literature, the skylark, nightingale, cuckoo, albatross and so on, remained more or less emblematic to me, and I learnt to recognize only those birds which are positively unavoidable, even by an unobservant suburbanite. But about wild flowers, moths, butterflies and even trees, I knew next to nothing, and about fungi, lichens, reptiles (apart from the vulgar and reckless toad), insects and other invertebrates, I knew nothing at all.

I exaggerate, but not much (for as a child I was fascinated

by zoos, circuses and the exploits of Armand and the bewitching Michaela Denis). In fact, my ignorance concerning British, or rather Welsh natural history is now something of a puzzle to me. With my parents, I spent long spells of my childhood on my grandfather's farm, which occupied a beautiful stretch of the south Pembrokeshire coast. Because of its exceptionally mild climate, on which my grandfather was then getting rich, that part of the world is famous, as I have since realized, for the abundance of its sea and coastal birds and its exotic flora. Day after day in the summer, we would walk through a meadow, through a wood, past freshwater ponds covered with lily pads where huge pike of fabulous antiquity were believed to lurk, across flats and reed beds that only flooded in winter, and onto the spectacular, cliff-bound dunes and beach of Broadhaven, a route which embraced at least five separate ecologies in the space of a couple of miles. Yet, despite the fact that my grandfather was a farmer and despite his friendship with Ronald Lockley, the great naturalist and writer, neither my cousins nor myself were ever shown the marvels that surrounded us or told their names. We grew up in utter ignorance of even the most rudimentary facts of animal behaviour and plant growth. In fairness, I must add that, notwithstanding my fantasies of accompanying Michaela Denis into the bush and becoming a mahout with 'Elephant' Bill in Burma, I never had the wit or initiative to investigate our unique environment on my own.

I write none of this in a spirit of bitterness. My family probably was less interested than most in natural history, but I suspect a larger force at work here. For reasons that are by no means clear to me, it seems that these mid-century generations, to which my parents and I belong, did not inherit the traditions and customs of their Victorian and Edwardian amateur naturalist ancestors, nor did they anticipate the eco-consciousness of the 1970s. I know that during these very years much important work was being done by specialists and academics in ethology, ecology and other disciplines, but it was not translated into the language of popular culture, and, speaking for the suburban circles in which I was brought up, I can only say that natural history possessed none of the charisma it does today. My public school, which so far as I can judge provided an adequate education in most respects, almost completely neglected environmental studies, as they would now be called. This generational lacuna has had its tragic consequences. If we had been more interested and better informed, we would perhaps have been quicker to notice the damage being done to the countryside by post-war agriculture, and would have resisted it more strenuously from the start. But, alas, protests were voiced only by a few isolated and largely unheard Jeremiahs. At least we can be sure that our children, who already know far more about these things than we ever did, will not allow what remains of the environment to be maltreated on the same scale.

At all events, typically or not, I grew up with a troglodytic unawareness of wild flowers, which if I noticed them at all, registered as no more than agreeable spots and splashes of colour occasionally glimpsed on the roadside, and instantly forgotten. Anything I know is the product of pedantic effort. In order to identify the most commonplace bloom, I am obliged to pick a specimen, take it back to my room and cluelessly go through my handbook from the beginning until I find a picture to match the wilting corpse on my desk. But then, and this is an exhilarating moment, a word that has forever been familiar but quite meaningless, except to signify 'flower' in the emptiest, most general sense, a word such as speedwell, campion, vetch or ragwort, suddenly becomes a living reality with its own particular and now unmistakeable colour, shape and season, its own vivid detail. By this simple means I enrich myself. A thing that has previously been nameless and unnameable, if mildly decorative, is transmogrified into knowledge, and, owing to some mysterious power of the imagination, the conversion from unknown to known has the effect of infinitely enhancing the plant's beauty. Botany, like all sciences, is at bottom inseparable from aesthetics.

Not always to their delight, I insist on taking my children with me on these botanical expeditions in the hope that, as adults, they will discover they have effortlessly imbibed their own personal flora. They will, I trust, know the names and characteristics of the contents of their vegetable and animal world as instinctively as they know those of their friends. In this respect, assuming I prove successful, they will, sadly, be exceptional. We no longer belong to a culture in which children, as a matter of course, grow up learning to name the parts of their ordinary physical universe. As far as wild flowers are concerned, they are less well known simply because they have become less common, herbicides having eliminated all but the most tenacious species from the verges and the remaining hedgerows. But the process whereby we have detached ourselves, both literally and intellectually, from the organic world has been going on far longer, and is not explicable in terms of a single cause. Our separation from nature is as much the result of cultural and philosophical changes as social and economic ones, and it certainly cannot be reduced to a simple consequence of the change from rural agriculture to urban industrialism. Country children, even those whose parents are members of the dwindling farming community, are hardly less ignorant about their natural surroundings than town children, and the tradition of knowing and using the properties of wild plants is all but dead, except among middle class revivalists, who for the most part have an urban background.

One of the most damaging paradoxes of our age is that whereas we, as a civilization, grow ever more knowledgeable about our planet and its universe, as individuals we become ever more dissociated from that knowledge. The vast increase in what might be called institutional knowledge, which has taken place during this century, has had the ironical effect of producing a complementary ignorance among the public. We know that things are known, and who knows them, but we ourselves know less and less, especially about the technology on which we rely more and more in our daily lives. The dimensions of our world are officially unveiled and handed down to us, and we, in our turn, passively receive the information and uncomprehendingly put it to use. We watch pictures on television of astronauts gambolling on the surface of the moon, and the topography of Mars grows as familiar as the sets of *Dallas* and *Dynasty*, but nowadays it is a rare person who can name the stars, and a far rarer one who can navigate by them. Or, to pick another example, medical care has now advanced to the point where the public can afford to know nothing about elementary first aid, and schools can afford to ignore it in their curricula. After weapons of war, our bodies have had more resources and research devoted to them than any other object of scientific enquiry, and as a result many of the thousand natural shocks that flesh is heir to are by and large curable or mendable, at least in the richer countries. All this is of course splendid, and I am not for a moment proposing Luddism in the face of either medical progress or any of the other great improvements in our material condition, which modern science has brought about. My point is, however, that these immense changes take place at a speed and with a decisiveness that leave both society and the individual incapable of absorbing them; the scope for personal initiative is reduced in direct proportion to the increase of professional knowledge. The alleviation of so many evils that have afflicted humanity for so many centuries has not comforted our spiritual confusion, which, if anything, has been aggravated, and that is the tragedy of our time.

I am convinced that our divorce from nature, though an inestimable boon in terms of setting us free from laborious toil, has nevertheless added to our sense of spiritual emptiness. The story of our alienation, to use a twentieth century word, turns out to have had its beginnings in a period well before the industrial revolution. The exodus from country to town appears to have been the result of intellectual, rather than technological developments. According to Keith Thomas, in his excellent *Man and the Natural World*, the change began in the sixteenth century, when people started to shake off what Thomas calls 'the breathtakingly anthropocentric spirit' in which medieval and Tudor thinking had interpreted the natural world.[1] Taking their authority from Genesis, preachers taught that animals and plants had been created exclusively for the use of Adam and his descendents, and that furthermore nature was specially tailored for his convenience. Thus, fish had been endowed with an instinct for swimming in shoals near the sea shore to make catching them easier, but wild animals had been exiled to uninhabited regions where they could do less harm. Horses and other domestic animals had been given variegated shapes and colours so that their owners might recognize them, though sheep and cattle had only been granted life in the first place to keep their meat fresh. Horse dung had been blessed with a sweet smell to prevent it from offending human noses. Not surprisingly, animal analogies occurred very often to a population mostly working in agriculture. Thomas tells us that during this early modern period, the official concept of the animal was a negative one, generally used to describe the opposite of what was held to be unique and admirable in the human species. The boundary between man and beast was felt to be dangerously fragile, 'bestial' being the term commonly applied to the physical vices, especially lust, but nonetheless animals, and to a lesser extent the rest of nature, provided a reference point for human self-definition, as well as an almost inexhaustible fund of symbolic meaning.

However, from the sixteenth century onwards this ancient vocabulary was gradually eroded by naturalists and farmers alike, who began to work out a much more detached, objective understanding of the natural world. The new scientific natural history of John Ray (1627–1705) and Linnaeus (1707–1778) destroyed the long-held notion that nature was responsive to human affairs; in place of a natural world fraught with symbolic overtones and sensitive to human behaviour, enlightened opinion proposed a separate natural scene, which could be dispassionately studied from outside. By the eighteenth century nature had been rendered a distinct sphere of existence, devoid of human significance.

The new science of natural history was stimulated by and, in its turn, made possible all sorts of improvements in agricultural efficiency, notably in the selective breeding of plants and animals. But, as Thomas emphasizes, this accretion of knowledge brought about loss as well as gain. Though food production was immeasurably increased, the slow, uneven and often most unscientific retreat from anthropocentrism left in its wake a painful sense of being displaced in the physical world, something no civilization had experienced before. Other peoples had felt they were the helpless victims of sadistic gods, but none had previously found themselves to be a species alien from nature. No sooner had we begun to demystify the natural world by classifying its parts and measuring its dimensions with telescope and microscope, than we realized we were isolated and anxious. And then the story took a strange twist: having convinced ourselves of our noble elevation above the brutes, we suddenly turned round and rushed to embrace them again. The age of scientific taxonomy was also the one which saw the first moves towards a campaign against cruelty to animals, together with the first stirrings of vegetarianism, the growth of pet-keeping on a large scale, and even the emergence of a belief in animal immortality. A similar pattern of non-utilitarian interest in plants and trees developed at the same time, and the expansion in flower gardening during the seventeenth and eighteenth centuries was on so large a scale as to be called a Gardening Revolution.

Nineteenth century science completed the separation of humanity from nature. Far from designing nature in accordance with human needs, God, it was slowly conceded, had played no part at all in its creation. Although Darwin's theory of evolution firmly instated the human species in the family of animals, the discovery that nature obeyed its own laws of development and followed its own time-scale finally made it impossible to invest the non-human world with any kind of preordained symbolic life. Thereafter, the most that could be exchanged with nature was a sense of reciprocity, a notion largely derived from Romanticism, which saw human emotion and experience reflected in natural phenomena, and allowed a feeling of continuity to flow between conscious, human thought and the independent, self-governing working of nature. By the twentieth century, anthropocentrism was being stood on its head: instead of seeing animals as emblems of human behaviour, Disney notwithstanding, we began to indulge in a sort of zoomorphism, whereby we tried to extract the essence of each animal and embody it in ourselves. This can be seen at its most extreme and preposterous in the kind of advertising which suggests that the lion's nobility and strength can be ingested by means of a chocolate bar, or that one's current account will magically assume the virility of a black stallion by placing it in a certain bank. Such is the sad iconography of envy.

The important thing revealed by our changing attitudes to nature is that our modern feeling of estrangement has its roots in the pre-industrial period, and is as much a product of our agricultural as our urban history. Moreoever, this sense of separation was the result of altering perceptions of nature, rather than literal removal from the countryside during the industrial revolution. It was an idea before it was a fact, and as such just as difficult to accept. The cultural accommodation of new perceptions of existence put forward by science is always painful, and is made doubly so by the absence of a connective religious or symbolic system, which can explain the 'progress' of civilization in terms that are more spiritually nourishing than the hollow rewards of productivity and profitability. However, the thrust of our historical development cannot be altered: like it or not, we are an urban industrial society, and, although the style of our industrial life may alter greatly, that in essence is what we are likely to remain for the next couple of generations at least. What we must do is to hold the line of damage, and struggle to repair our existing relations; for it is consolation in the here and now that we require. I believe that our relations with nature, if not with each other, are capable of improvement within the scope of our present resources. Since, as we have seen, the evolution of our attitudes to nature was caused by new perceptions no less than new technologies and new economic forces, we presumably have it in our power to change our perceptions again. Or, rather, we have the power to change our perception of ourselves by rediscovering the roots of our being in nature. And by nature I mean here whatever aspect of the natural scene is accessible and suits the individual's taste; the weed at the back door, or Wordsworth's Grasmere.

An essential feature of humanity is the desire to investigate the physical world, to test its properties, and to name its parts – activities which bring quite as much psychological satisfaction as practical benefit, and help us make sense as well as use of our universe. But although this desire is badly frustrated, the countryside, or indeed any patch of wild growth, still offers people the opportunity to explore and enquire, using their own initiative, satisfying their own whims. Wild plants are common property, a strand of nature's living tissue which is accessible to everybody. They are not the product of computer, laboratory, factory or farm; they are not exclusive to the rich, the expert, the educated or even the countryman; nor are they the exotic souvenir of some other climate brought back by houseplant importers. Unlike every other natural material we eat or use, they have not been processed. We have lost contact with the beasts whose flesh we eat, the trees whose fruit we eat, and the plants and animals that clothe us, but with wild plants we can still gratify our ancient, inborn urge to sniff, prod, taste, turn over and tear apart, play with, cook, wear, display, carve, weave, build with and generally satisfy our curiosity about things that interest us. Our wilderness may have shrunk, and may only survive in reserves, but its plants are genuinely wild, for all that. However decorative, house plants, like pets, are prisoners; wild plants, on the other hand, grow where they will and must be discovered where they are. To that degree, they are, in their unassuming way, subversive, and the business of finding them is a mild act of subversion, for it means stepping for a moment outside the regulated paths of consumer life. Though wild plants can be sold, they are, by definition, independent of the market.

The countryside continues to give people the chance to measure their relative stature and discover what might be called their metaphysical bearings. For some people, their sense of personal significance is restored, paradoxically, by contemplating what used to be called the sublime, that is, the awesome and vast in nature: scenery dominated by cosmic natural forces which also confirms the inconsequence of mankind. The sublime induces an ecstasy, a sense of fusing with the universe, of transcendence, and these feelings often inspire an intensity of conviction in religious minds. The sublime has its democratic side too: ever since the scale of human systems has threatened to crush the individual, there has been a taste for landscape which made human attainments look insignificant in relation to nature's omnipotence. This contrast dignifies the individual by making everyone equal: to the ocean all men and women, governors and governed alike, are less than fish.

But, for other people, smaller pleasures bring greater consolation, and it is the alpine flower, instead of towering summits, beetling crags and yawning chasms, that moves them most. John Ruskin declared that flowers have no sublimity, because they do not provoke awe and sorrow, which are at the root of the sublime sensation. He also saw a wide difference between flower-loving minds and minds 'of the highest order'. His words are worth quoting:

Flowers seem intended for the solace of ordinary humanity: children love them; quiet, tender, contented ordinary people love them as they grow; luxurious and disorderly people rejoice in them gathered: They are the cottager's treasure . . . Passionate or religious minds contemplate them with fond, feverish intensity . . . To the child and the girl, the peasant and the manufacturing operative, to the grisette and the nun, the lover and monk, they are precious always. But to the men of supreme power and thoughtfulness, precious only at times; symbolically and pathetically often to the poets, but rarely for their own sake. They fall forgotten from the great workmen's and soldier's hands. Such men will take, in thankfulness, crowns of leaves, or crowns of thorns – not crowns of flowers.

Not being a man of supreme power and thoughtfulness myself, I am happy to count myself among the ranks of monks, grisettes and other members of ordinary humanity, and acknowledge the truth of what he says on our behalf. Though his way of expressing himself may seen condescending, Ruskin has nonetheless put his finger on the varieties of appeal flowers have for many people. But for us today they provide another pleasure, which is also small in scale, though profound in its implications. To match a wild flower with its picture in the flora, and give a name to something hitherto unknown, is to break free from the cage of artificiality that threatens to confine our imaginations, and claim a piece of the universe for ourselves. This leap from the abstract to the real, from a printed image to its living original, reinforces the link that joins art to nature, a link which is perpetually strained as our personal creativity dwindles and our minds are washed grey by television soap.

As Ruskin suggested, flowers yield a surprising range of emotional satisfactions. By taking flowers seriously, by studying them closely, perhaps drawing or painting them, one becomes engaged in an activity at once scientific and aesthetic. The beauty of a plant growing half-concealed in the grass, a mere dot of animated colour casually appreciated while one walks by, fulfills its promise a hundredfold when carefully examined. Here are the workings of biology, the very mechanics of reproduction, laid bare for anyone to see, but illustrated in colours that dazzle the eye with their purity. Take the bugle, for instance, that 'most lovable and inexhaustible plant', as Geoffrey Grigson once called it, which parades like a disorderly regiment in the cleared spaces of our wood during the last weeks of May. Its corolla has five petals of a glorious violet-blue, two forming a very short, jagged upper lip, and the others forming a long, three-lobed lower lip, which curves and droops. Standing just below the upper lip, and arching over the lower lip, are four vivid yellow stamens, the pollen-bearing male organs, and beside them a single style, where the pollen germinates after the wind has blown it across the teeming gap. What could be simpler, clearer, more graphically explicit? And what could be lovelier?

It is not sentimentality alone that makes people choose flower books illustrated by Victorian ladies and clergymen in favour of those illustrated with modern colour photographs. The fact is that photographs of wild flowers, no matter how sophisticated in technique, fail to do justice to them, but watercolour studies at their best, and many of the best were painted by amateurs in the nineteenth century, do succeed in bringing out their essential qualities. Photographs tend to flatten the plant into two dimensions and coat its colours with a false glossiness; however, their real fault is, ironically, that they allow no room for artifice. The water colour sketch, on the other hand, is the classic medium just because it is the product of a highly unnatural process. Owing to a very long national tradition of painting flowers, stretching back to the middle ages, we are used to pictures which are a combination of art and botanical illustration, and we expect to see the plant subject arranged on the paper in such a way as to display its various parts, even if this involves a distortion of nature. We expect the water-colourist to pin the specimen to his board, manipulate it into a position that is simultaneously artistic, natural and informative, and still keep the juice flowing through its veins. Not only that, but we also look for an emotional response to the plant's particular character. (The recently discovered *Frampton Flora*, introduced by Richard Mabey, is an excellent instance of this blend of feeling and precision, which is peculiar to natural history art.) The photograph cannot answer these conflicting demands, and so the flower guide remains one of the last bastions of painterly skill to defy the domination of photographs in book illustration.

Wild flowers are so profuse, so unpretentious, and yet so exquisite, it is difficult not to think of them as sheer decoration, a gratuitous ornament, scattered like jewellery over the body of ordinary nature. But, unlike precious stones, flowers fade and die, leaving the plain greenery of their plants for the eye of the botanist alone, until they too perish and only their roots and rhizomes prevail, invisibly storing growth for the next year. The season of their 'glory in the flower' is poignantly brief: during the month or so I have taken to write this chapter the dense cushion of colour we all admired on that sunny day in mid-May has completely changed, and is now a dishevelled bush of green, dominated by grasses which are beginning to seed. The anemones and celandines have entirely disappeared; the ground ivy has lost its miniature compactness and has grown to a straggling foot, or foot and a half, with a few stale blooms stuck to its gangling stems; the dog's mercury has been overwhelmed by the grass, and only the brambles, now mostly upright and fresh with new life, mark the site of our sampler of May flowers. Nearby, in a swampy patch of open ground, the bugle still stands in ragged ranks, but its uniform is threadbare, the gold braid of its stamens has dried to nothing, and its brave blue petals have bleached and shrivelled.

The fleeting inflorescence of these little plants serves as a melancholy reminder of our own short span, but it is also an assurance of the perennial endurance of natural life, of which we are an outgrowth. Because of their quicksilver transience, wild flowers hold a special appeal for us. Our contradictory nature is such that while we crave permanence, tradition, the long flow of things, and all the other slow-footed patterns we invent to give us the illusion of damming time, or at least of slowing our headlong rush to the grave, we also have an insatiable appetite for novelty, change and variety. This peculiar conflict of desires is uniquely satisfied by the quick coming and going of wild flowers. Each month sees a rash of new blooms, which dazzle us for a moment, and then expire, making way for some fresh marvel. But though these flickers of sexual display may be swift, the species that produce them have been doing so, year by year, all our lives. They have flourished for century after century; indeed, many have occupied this island since it was colonized by megalithic man, who, no doubt, also picked, sniffed and chewed them – and put them behind his ear.

This eternal flow of death and rebirth puts us in touch with a system of time that is very different from the chaos of shocks, alarms and defeats that makes up our history. The ebb and flow of natural time helps us to endure, and to preserve those things which are most severely tested by history's cruel disorderliness, but which must survive if we are to redeem ourselves. Renewal in nature refreshes our humanity, making it that much easier to hold fast to our principles and keep our hope green.

VILLAGE GOTHIC

The day has nearly ended. I am walking down the little street (prosaically known as 'The Street') that forms the crooked spine of the old village. A gaudy October sunset has spattered the sky with streaks of purple and orange, and a ragged fog is coiling off the paddock, driving the ponderous pink sows back to their sty. Lights are glowing in most cottages, outshining the sun's dying clinker, while smoke from their chimneys thickens the mist. The road rises gently towards a knoll where the church stands, making it a prominent landmark, visible from almost every quarter of the village.

Standing at the postbox and looking across the road at the spreading black shapes of the yew trees, I decide to go into the church. In the graveyard only the most recent headstones, which are made of clean white marble not yet stuccoed with lichen, catch the last of the light. The tower above me is a looming dark mass and I can only just make out the chequerboard patterns of flints decorating the walls of the porch.

I fumble for the keyhole and turn the heavy lock. As I push open the door I feel on my face a slight rush of colder air, whose smell I would recognize blindfold. Inside, it is quite dark and I walk gingerly towards the curtained vestry below the west window. Despite my caution, I crack my shin against the lid of the long, iron-bound treasure chest which is displayed in the nave, though it holds nothing more valuable than an ancient vacuum cleaner. Having found the panel of switches, I use both hands to turn them all on together and suddenly the whole building seems to leap to its feet as the nave is charged with light. Outside, people must be wondering what is going on, for now the church is glowing in the night like a huge lantern.

Since moving to the village ten years ago, I have come to love this church – St George's. Built more or less at one time, around 1400, and restored heavily by William Butterfield in the late nineteenth century, it is a fine example of perpendicular. Like many other churches in Suffolk, it looks an absurdly grandiose edifice for so small a community, and, to tell the truth, its massive, somewhat martial tower is not to my taste. But once inside I always know that my attachment is not just the result of parochial loyalty. For a parish church, its nave is unusually tall, with long, elegant windows. Having no aisles it is narrow too, but very graceful in all its proportions. As with any church of its age, it has many intriguing features, but its wooden furnishings and carvings make it remarkable even by the standards of this county of remarkable churches.

Standing on the arm of each bench end is a small carved figure, roughly the span of an adult hand in height. The figures date from the second half of the fifteenth century and there are no less than 66 in all, every one different. However, they need careful inspection because the rubbing of multitudinous hands over five centuries has darkened and polished the oak and smoothed out much of the carving detail, giving them a false look of uniformity. The subject matter of these figures is indiscriminately drawn from Christian symbolism, medieval bestiaries and nature. In the porch, for example, four angels are roosting like a flock of orderly birds, their wings folded demurely behind them. Just inside the door, a battered little mermaid still gamely flaunts herself. Near her is a bearded camel whose hump has slipped down to its tail. You can also see a pair of pigs, one with sinister human feet, the other sweetly playing a harp. Here is a strange, sad, armless woman and there a monstrous man whose head grows out of his stomach. In the shadows, Gossip dips her quill in a bottle of poison. And what is this? A sharp beak, wings, talons and a coiling, reptilian tail: it can only be the fearsome cockatrice, which is hatched from the egg of a seven-year-old cock laid on a dunghill and incubated by a toad.

This bizarre menagerie is by no means the only carving to be found. In fact, almost every wooden surface is carved or decorated; some would have been painted in pre-Reformation days. The backs and ends of the benches themselves are carved in handsome, flowing patterns. The tops of the bench ends, known as poppy-heads, are carved too, mostly in the shape of foliage, which seems to curl and spring out of the wood as if sap still flowed in the old oak. Predictably, the most elaborate carving is reserved for the chancel stalls where the clergy sat, hidden from the congregation by the rood screen. Every part of these stalls and their desks is crusted and enriched with carvings, which are like wooden jewels, their polished facets gleaming darkly in the soft light. The end of one stall is especially beautiful, being carved in tracery reminiscent of the most ornate perpendicular windows. The undersides of the stall seats are equipped with misericords – the little shelves on which priests could rest their buttocks during arduously long services without appearing to sit down – and these show the winged lion of St Mark and the winged bull of St Luke. The finials on the desks are tall and delicate, like the nave itself, and depict priests and servers dressed for mass, together with a preacher in his pulpit. Behind the stalls is the dado, a sort of low fence dividing the nave from the chancel, and all that is left of the rood screen. It is only simply carved, but is painted in its original medieval colours of green and red, which remind me of the green yews outside in the graveyard and their bright red autumn berries.

All these works of art have given me enormous pleasure over the last ten years and hardly a fortnight has gone by without my walking up the street to look at them again. Whenever I go inside the church, whether alone or to show it to other people, I always feel soothed and heartened. No other building I know has the same power to restore.

However, none of this is to imply a dawning of faith. On the contrary, though it may seem perversely ungrateful, one of the paradoxical effects of my becoming an habitual 'church crawler' is that my lifelong atheism has, if anything, been confirmed. Nonetheless, I like to think of myself as more than a mere tourist when visiting a church; I am, instead, a secular pilgrim. Our magnificent Suffolk churches, with their stout, conspicuous towers, their lavish porches and angel roofs, their flint flushwork and airy clerestories, their flamboyant font covers and absurd fauna, are all for me primarily aesthetic objects, whose religious significance is of great, but strictly academic, interest. And yet the emotions they arouse are both complex and profound, and are a direct response to the religious essence of the church and its symbolism. Or rather, they are a response to these great themes of existence – birth, marriage, morality and, above all, the mystery of death – which are the special province of all religions. In our culture, churches are still the most complete expression of those themes, even for an atheist.

The church moves me too because it unifies the village and its landscape in a single, reciprocal creation. The materials from which it is built, notably the flint outside and the oak within, were of course taken from local sources, probably from the parish itself where they still exist in great profusion. Indeed, I would guess that today there are even larger numbers of mature oaks than there were when the church was being furnished in the fifteenth century. As for the flint, its clay-white skulls and bones continue everywhere to push up through the soil like a gruesome, never-failing crop. Most of the older garden walls in the village are made of flint topped with rotund brick copings, and they seem to draw their cool blue-grey tones, flecked with white and ochre, from our wind-blown Suffolk skies. When the walls begin to crumble, they shed a rubble of loose nodules which become indistinguishable from the flints rising for the first time out of their earth womb. These stones bind the cottages to the land they stand on. The village has roots of flint.

The church's salient position on the skyline marries the community with its countryside, while pointing to transcendent aspirations, an idea Constable put to masterly use in his paintings of the Stour valley in which Dedham church is an inevitable feature. The original builders of medieval churches intended them to be enclosed and segregated places devoted to the worship of God. Nature and the world were rigorously excluded. Natural light was only allowed to enter through the mediation of stained glass and its sacred imagery, leaving no view of the secular world visible from within. Natural forms were acceptable as the basis of ornament only after they had been invested with spiritual significance. It was the essence of Gothic that each scrap of foliage, each piece of knapped flint, each floor tile, even the waterspouts on the gutters, should be loaded with symbolic meaning. Yet, ironically, one of the qualities that most appeals to our modern taste in Gothic decoration is precisely the free-flowing exchange we see between the artistic and the organic, between natural life outside and its re-creation inside, between local raw materials and their expressive use in construction. Far from being sequestered, the church fuses with its surrounding countryside as no other building does.

The church acts as a monument to the story of the village and the inextricable twining together of people and their place. Our present landscape is in fact essentially a nineteenth century one, though its Victorian beard has been shaved off. Hedgerows have been grubbed up, fields have been joined together to form steppes of barley and wheat, the little river has been canalized and its marshy banks have been drained, the post office has surrendered and gone, and bungalows encroach on the churchyard. But for all that the lineaments of the village and its encircling farm land have not been radically changed since the 1850s when the present Hall was built and its park landscaped.

To stand on the terrace of Stowlangtoft Hall, which incidentally is now a nursing home for old people, and let your eye stroll round its wooded parkland, its ornamental lake and pheasant copses, and take a few steps down the trundling lane that leads to the village, is to see the landscape as it was designed to be seen. To survey this elegant prospect is also to realize with what finely-calculated care our part of the countryside was shaped and decorated. It comes as a shock to discover that our natural surroundings were once as deliberately planned as a bridge or railway engine might have been. As it happens, our old house stands directly opposite the Hall on the margin of the park, which gave us a stagehand's outlook, for we saw the vista in reverse.

I do not write in a spirit of resentment, far less of Jacobin frustration. Although I am as alert as the next man to the evils of private property, I nonetheless believe that everyone in the village has good cause to be grateful to the family which built the Hall and whose bodies now lie beneath locked slate doors in an untended sepulchre behind the church. Naturally, these people planted out their estate chiefly for the benefit of their own descendents, of whom none remain in the parish, but at least they did so in an open-handed way, on a grand scale affecting the whole village, and in the knowledge that generations of the family would have to be carried down the steps into that slate sepulchre before their landscaping achieved full maturity. Nor was their faith misplaced. There may be parts of Suffolk that are more spectacular, there are certainly more picturesque parts, but I know of nowhere else that is so subtly, so serenely beautiful.

The glory of the estate is its trees, which can be seen growing in great abundance and variety from every road and path, and, I imagine, from almost every window. The skyline is everywhere fringed with spinneys and larger tracts of wood, and all the fields within sight of the Hall are classically enhanced with rings of towering pine, curtains of willow, or single specimens of oak and elm. This enviable largesse of trees owes its survival to the present owners of the estate, who are shooting enthusiasts and have kept their woodland intact both for the sake of its aesthetic value and to give cover to their breeding pheasants. However, by a peculiarly modern irony, the very force that is preserving our generously wooded landscape is at the same time alienating us from it. As is usual on a shooting estate, the 'public' is discouraged from entering any of the covers for fear of disturbing the game. Thus we, the non-shooting village, find ourselves in the odd position of being surrounded by lovely countryside, yet being unable to walk in it, for apart from a couple of footpaths we are confined to the roads.

This exclusion of the public is no more than the owners' right, but it adds to the importance of the church. Every village church bears witness to another history, an alternative tradition of ordinary people that is not stamped with the

badge of a single owner, or at least not as conspicuously as the landscape. And in small, one-time agricultural communities like ours, the church resists the pervading presence of ownership which tends to haunt them even after the big house has been deserted and sold up. It is true that in their way trees also defy ownership, because no matter how rich a landowner may be, he cannot do much to shape or influence the growth of a tree once he has planted it. He can only watch and wait with the rest of us. Its quirks of form, its colours and changeability, all belong to nature, while its aesthetic appeal belongs to anyone who cares to appreciate it. However, although a tree's beauty may transcend property, its existence remains, potentially at least, a matter of business, and deforestation is big business. Now, churches are not invulnerable to the ravages of the market either, but as long as a building is consecrated it is effectively common property. And it is not only visible, but accessible to everybody – Christians, atheists and the indifferent.

Apart from the country seat and the occasional domesticated castle, no other kind of building offers the same testament to endurance in the face of change and by means of change. Like the parish church, the country house is often the result of many alterations and additions accumulating over a long stretch of time, each new stratum registering a swing of taste, a rise in family fortunes or perhaps the sheer eccentricity of some owner. A Jacobean hall may have been masked by a neo-classical façade or a Victorian glasshouse attached to a Regency drawing room, and yet such seemingly incompatible elements often amount to a surprisingly coherent or, at any rate, a satisfying whole. More even than the intrinsic beauty of the house and the rarity of its contents, it is the visible record of gradual accretion through the ages, the piling up of goods layer by layer, that makes the country house so compelling. Individuals may come and go, but each generation inherits more from the last and passes on still more to the next. Thus, the family prevails and dispossessing mortality is defied.

The great difference between the church and the country house, in this respect, is that the latter is designed above all to broadcast and celebrate the continuity of private owner- ship. The family crest is literally or implicitly emblazoned on every curtain, moulding and mantelpiece. In effect, a secular symbolism is at work, using very similar means of expression to those found inside a Gothic church. Each artefact and decoration is designed to magnify the glory of the dynasty, instead of God, and nothing is allowed to dim or obscure its prestige. Rather than pictures of Our Lord, the Holy Family and the saints, the walls are hung with portraits of the present lord, his family and illustrious forebears.

Perhaps the analogy cannot be taken too far. In any case, I am certainly not trying to extol the virtues of feudalism and Gothic at the expense of country house capitalism and its art. Both social systems were oppressive and exploitative in their different ways, and both have produced their distinctive art forms, which we admire and treasure today. However, despite the fact that all aristocratic collections contain works of art, notably their paintings, which point to values and priorities in direct conflict with the ethos of the house, I am still drawn to the deeper, homogenous symbolism that gives life to a Gothic church.

While being an atheist sets a certain limit on one's appreciation of any church, Gothic or otherwise, it does not mean that one's response is necessarily confined to the lowest level of aesthetic pleasure. Belief is not a qualification without which one is debarred from being moved by church architecture, or for that matter by sacred music, paintings of the Crucifixion or even by the Bible itself. (At the top of my personal desert island selection would be Haydn's music for *The Seven Last Words of Christ on the Cross*, which is the most intense declaration of faith in music I know.) A secular audience is capable of being deeply affected by religious works of art because these works use particular, highly-charged images in order to express themes and emotions which are common to all human experience. Paradoxically, works of art that spring from the most elaborate and authoritative symbolic systems are the ones which retain the greatest power to speak across history and culture, and stir people from very different backgrounds. Thus, it is the very rootedness of parish Gothic in an all-inclusive symbolic world which ensures that it continues to hold profound aesthetic significance for its modern, largely infidel admirers.

The more I study churches the more I am struck by the close affinity between nature and the Gothic style, and this gives me a vital bridge from medieval to modern, from sacred to secular. The way in which carving, paint and ornament break out to adorn every surface and fill every crevice, sometimes densely and massively in a small place, sometimes with fantastic elaboration in a plain setting, and sometimes leaving bald spaces where ornamentation might have been expected – the way this random abundance spreads and swarms irresistibly recalls the way in which the life force drives lichen, ivy, mistletoe and a host of other organisms cling and climb, root and sprout across the bark of big trees and among their branches. In short, Gothic seems to share with nature an irrepressible impulse for growth. An energy as vigorous as the power that animates the organic world quickens its timber and stone.

And there is another, more abstract similarity. In his second collection of essays on natural history, Stephen Jay Gould describes how as a boy his interest in dinosaurs and the retrieval of their bones led him to stumble upon the theory of evolution. 'Ever since then,' he writes, 'the duality of natural history – richness in particularities and potential union in underlying explanation – has propelled me.'[1] Despite the seemingly infinite range of forms in which plants and animals have been shaped by adaptation, the working of evolution is subject to a relatively small set of unifying laws. As it happens, Gothic is informed by the same kind of dualism as Gould noted: it encouraged a teeming diversity of decorative and functional form, but insisted that every part should nonetheless contribute to a very small core of theological ideas. Symbol was piled on symbol; everything meant something else and nothing was without its sacred significance. Yet, though the range of symbolic material was extensive, the matrix of meaning remained severely concentrated. For example, the choice of creatures suitable for use as symbols was as wide as local fauna and the bestiaries could suggest, and medieval churches are therefore crowded out with lambs, sheep, rams, kids, calves, pelicans, lions, serpents, worms and eagles, among many others. However, this zoological latitude only provided the means of saying the same thing in many ways: all the creatures in my list were symbols of Christ, or some aspect of his being. These creatures respectively symbolized Christ's innocence, patience, leadership, likeness to sinful flesh, sacrifice for mankind, redemption, kingship and courage, death and wisdom, resurrection, and ascension.

I am not trying to claim that Gothic is superior to other architectural traditions – though I personally find it to be so – but by favouring variety over elegance, and spontaneity over formalism, Gothic does provide a uniquely fitting metaphor for natural life. In my eyes, our village church stands as testimony to our human capacity for harmonizing the disparate, while yet allowing diversity to spring from unity. And these are qualities which almost define the activity of nature. By the same token, the church as a work of art is a symbol of what we must at all costs preserve in the countryside and rediscover in ourselves. Neither Christianity nor Gothic can be revived, but their very occurrence in history, and the long passage of their dominance, show that the human imagination is able to create on a scale that rivals nature in coherence no less than beauty.

WHO OWNS NATURE?

Nowadays, whenever I make one of my rare visits to London I feel a terrific sense of exhilaration as I step off the train at Liverpool Street. I rejoice in the grime, I breathe in the intoxicating smog, my feet dance across the unfamiliar, blackened concrete and I throw myself into the throng of bodies streaming down the stairs to the Underground. The noise, crowds and dirt, the ceaseless agitation of vehicles and people, the chic women, the towering buildings, the whirling lights and the profusion and variety of things to buy, especially books – all these shout 'London' to me, or whisper it bewitchingly, and in the classic fashion of bumpkins I am both foolish with excitement and a little frightened.

Needless to say, as the day goes by this rustic jubilance slowly gives way to disillusionment. Weary and jaded, sour and spent-up, guilty and half-drunk, I sink into my seat on the train going home and swear I will never set foot in that madhouse again. And as the view beyond the rushing carriage window gradually turns green, no pastoral cliché seems too banal to describe the freshness, the tranquillity, the sheer friendliness of the East Anglian countryside.

However, to go back to the beginning of the adventure, one of the many factors contributing to my naive elation is the knowledge that I am to be liberated for a little while from the constraints of private property. Now, this may

71

sound perverse. After all, in London, or in Bury St Edmunds for that matter, every street bellows the names of its various owners at you: the names of shops, cinemas, restaurants, businesses, institutions and so on are all blazoned in lights and lettering from every door and window. The badges of property are ubiquitous and inescapable. Here at home, on the other hand, I can look out from my house over hundreds of acres of farm and woodland, all of it very lovely, with not a single sign or notice in view. And yet, like anyone else living here, I know the geography of these estates and farms well and I can put a name to every quarter of the view. Except for the roads and a footpath or two, all the land we can see is privately owned and in the country, ownership means exclusion. We country people are condemned to be voyeurs, for we are surrounded by the beautiful, which we may not touch, far less penetrate.

In London or any other city it is, as I say, different. There, property, at least at street level, is designed to seduce and draw you in. The architect's job is to make his client's shop or bank look as inviting and alluring as possible. On a city street, nobody is a trespasser: private property is open to all. It goes without saying that this hospitality is entirely commercial in motive and that its limitations are soon reached, but it does have the effect of giving city dwellers a credible sense of owning their city. In a very real way, Londoners own Selfridges as much as the National Gallery or Hyde Park. However, although country people may share this feeling of notional ownership in relation to their village, they can never do so in relation to the surrounding farm land.

And it is for this reason that I feel oppressed by the rule of property here in the countryside. The relief I experience on the platform at Liverpool Street is not to be had in Bury St Edmunds, or any of the other small market towns roundabout, where the influence of our modern squirearchy continues to impinge. The mode of ownership conceded to farmers seems to be very extensive, almost absolute. Indeed, they may be said even to own nature itself.

At first sight, the idea of anyone owning nature appears to be an offensive contradiction in terms. Ownership is an artificial convention and nature is above and beyond our sordid human arrangements. How can the agility of a swift be owned? Or the irridescence of a damselfly belong to one person and not another? If I were to say, 'these are *my* badgers', it would not only sound mean and grasping, but would have the ring of megalomania as well. The next logical step would be to proclaim, 'my clouds . . . my rainbow . . . my sunset'. Badgers are free and independent creatures, wherever they may happen to dig their sets, and they cannot be branded with anyone's name. And rainbows have yet to be privatized.

The essence of nature is surely that it cannot be owned. We value it precisely according to its lack of value in the marketplace. Nature cannot be reified, cannot be diminished to sets of things. To reduce it to property, worse still to a commodity that can be bought and sold for profit, is to denature nature.

Yet, to talk like this is to denature nature by another method, namely, by mystifying it. If property is a convention, so too is nature, at any rate in the sense that I am using here. The word 'nature', amongst other things, denotes the difference between the world of our making, including agriculture, and the wild, untouched, autonomous world of plants and animals co-existing with ours. But, as such, the term defines a myth; at least, sadly, it is a myth in Britain today. It is no co-incidence that the word acquired this shade of meaning in the late eighteenth century, at the very time when it was first realized that the independence of that other, non-human world was being threatened. The fact is that human beings and nature are no longer residents of a common environment, for nature has been demoted and is now our dependant. The real contradiction, if you like, is that the wildness of our wildlife has become a privilege which could be withdrawn at any moment. Paradoxically, to be wild now means to be in need of protection, for the spontaneity of nature has to be carefully supervised. The dictionary definition of *wild* refers to an animal living in a state of nature, but it is the highly problematic state of nature that is causing so much concern. Nature can no longer be taken for granted, a fact which presumably calls for its meaning to be redefined as well. The truth is that nature has become our responsibility and, to that degree, it is also our property. We have inverted the medieval, biblical belief that nature was created for our use and pleasure; we humans are its creators now and it is we who must provide for nature's needs.

Let us come down to earth. All species of plants and animals depend on land or water for their habitats, breeding grounds, nesting sites and so on, and, since in this country every acre of land and water is somebody's property, nature is effectively owned in certain very practical respects. And because about 78 per cent of Britain's surface is under some sort of agriculture, it follows that by and large, nature is owned by farmers. The other great proprietors of nature are of course the trusts, societies and public agencies which hold land for conservation purposes, and they, after all, buy their properties with the express intention of stopping anyone else, particularly farmers, from owning them.

On a small, highly cultivated, densely populated island such as ours, nature can hardly avoid being owned. The problem, however, is not to liberate nature from ownership, but on the contrary to ensure that the present generation of landowners treats kindly the natural and the historical heritage which is bound to fall into its care. Alas, as we all know, today's farmers tend not to be the benign stewards of pastoral myth. Ownership of four-fifths of the country is being concentrated in the hands of fewer and fewer people, whose activities are not easily controlled by law, whose methods are inimical to conservation, and whose handsome income is largely derived from public money. And it is our money therefore which makes it possible for them to go on 'improving' their land, as the laughable euphemism has it, while in the process ruining the countryside. For although nature may, in the strictest sense, belong to nobody, the countryside, which is an entirely social and cultural concept, belongs to everybody. In short, it may be their land, but it is *our* countryside.

The question of ownership in respect of nature turns out to be more complicated than might have been expected. How far do farmers' rights extend? Or is it simply that nature is in their power and the rest of us have no choice but to hope they will undergo a change of heart and repent? The law, in the shape of the Wildlife and Countryside legislation, does place limitations on rights of farmers, but in practice these are only observed by an admirable minority, while the rest understandably take advantage of the very lucrative chances offered to them by government to work their land still more intensively. My own belief is that the key to conservation does not lie in tightening up planning restrictions, or in devising stricter codes of behaviour, but in reconstructing the economics of the farming industry. Apart from anything else, a reduction in the level of protection given to large farmers would bring about a radical change in the structure of ownership. The smaller farmer would return to the countryside, land would be less exhaustively cultivated, and the consumer would benefit no less than the environment.

Nothing will reform the countryside as effectively as reforming the balance of ownership.

But there are other, ecological considerations which are impossible to regulate by either law or economics. For instance, the whole point of farming, which is to confine and control growth, flies in the teeth of nature. The good seed is *not* scattered on the land, it is drilled in very frugally and precisely. Nor is it by any means God's Almighty Hand that feeds and waters the seed once it is planted. The farmer uses every aid with which a highly sophisticated industry can supply him in order to maximize his crop. Agriculture and nature are opposed to each other, and always have been; only pastoral romanticism sees the farmer and nature harmoniously yoked together. It is not possible to work in harmony with the blowfly, the thistle or liver fluke; they must be ruthlessly eliminated.

By the same token, the field, the fundamental unit of farming, is not a natural feature determined by geography. It is a thoroughly artificial product, whose boundaries are drawn by law, custom and the caprices of the property market. Respect for these boundaries is quite as important to the farmer as what goes on within them. The hedge, the fence and ditch are lines, both practical and symbolic, which the farmer must trace round his property before he can get to work. Thus, agriculture contains while nature expands. However, the great principle of ecology is that no organism exists in isolation or independence. There is no such thing as freedom in nature, but there is no alienation either. Every plant and creature is attached, at some point, to an extended chain of dependence and exploitation.

Needless to say, ecology is no respecter of property. Its notion of territory is very different from an estate agent's and it deals in dimensions of time and space that would unhinge the sharpest lawyer. These webs of interdependence embrace water, earth and air; they connect together birds, reptiles, fish, insects and mammals, as well as every species of plant, with all their differing time-scales of existence and variable needs, season by season. Nobody can own these ecological systems; they will not submit to jurisprudence. There is a unity in nature that transcends the partitioning of property. And it is exactly this far-flung coherence unifying elms, rooks, storm-clouds and mud in a single, inclusive sweep of biological life, that transforms farmland into countryside. Agriculture is land treated economically, but the idea of countryside treats land aesthetically and fuses the subdivisions of property into the wholeness of landscape.

No one who owns a car, a house or even a picture supposes that he has the right to do what he likes with it, but owing to their particular historical background, farmers have come to think that the rights conferred on them by ownership are unconditional. As it happens, I sympathize with this, because as a basis for agriculture it seems reasonable and practical. But, as we have seen, even the largest landowner cannot claim to own the ecology attached to his property; he only owns, if that is the word, odd bits and links of these wonderfully ramifying chains of interdependence. A farmer may fairly assert that he owns his pond, but he does not own its pond life, the heron which visits to fish or the tree it nests in. By draining his pond he is not only killing a multitude of individual organisms, but destroying a complex natural system over which he has no rights at all.

In fact, this simple principle of restricted ownership is recognized by farmers in other respects. For example, it is accepted that although you may own both banks of a river this does not give you the right to pollute the water flowing between them. But this principle must somehow be extended to nature at large, because plants and animals are bound together in ecological unions as surely as molecules of water flow together to form rivers. Ecology obeys its own laws and cannot, even for the sake of its own health, submit to legal convenience. Likewise, our aesthetic perceptions are quite insensitive to the patterns made by property. The eye cannot be confined or repulsed by gates and walls; it is an incorrigible trespasser and, to that degree, our aesthetic response to the countryside is always potentially subversive. A farmer may own every acre of land as far as the horizon in every direction, but he still does not own the view. Landscape is common property. Or, to put it the other way round, there is no land so private it cannot be poached by the inquisitive eye.

As I have tried to show, trees and churches also defy the authority of property and every parish has within it some such feature which bears witness to experience outside the control of ownership. All but the most rationalized land-scapes contain places and sights around which all sorts of private and communal associations gather. These landmarks may be spectacular or humble, they may be natural or artificial, historical or transient, but between them they make up the meaning of the countryside. They cleave together in a kind of ecology of the imagination, which links farming with nature, property with beauty, community with landscape, and transcends them all. This imaginative coherence reveals the continuities of life and death in human history, no less than in nature, and the flow of experience is rendered meaningful.

Nature will never be property, but all of us can appropriate its symbolic suggestiveness. As biological beings ourselves, we can hardly fail to see our own sensual life reflected in that of other organisms. The symbolism of nature is our creation and, in this poetic sense, the natural world is a universal possession: we all own it. And so, when farmers put nature to death, and governments pay them to do so, they not only kill what does not belong to them, they also strike a blow directly at our imagination which is the essence of our nature.

THE POETRY OF BIRDS

Each spring our conker tree throws out a short beard of new
growth from the many fruitful burrs and knobs on its trunk,
and if these shoots were allowed to grow they would rapidly
acquire the strength and stature of saplings. This year, as I
was clipping off the fresh bristles with secateurs, I came
across a small, neat nest built on a platform of leaf stems
about three and a half feet off the ground. It was so well
concealed that I had cut off one of its supports before I
noticed the edge of its little moss-bound wall. Though
wonderfully disguised, it was nevertheless in a very vulnerable
position, for it was built on the north side of the trunk,
which meant it was shaded from the sun, but was directly
opposite the front door and well within the reach of our
curious children. The nest was empty, but must have been
newly made, because the leaves on which it stood were only
a few inches long in the stem and were still developing fast,
giving it extra protection and stability with every day's
growth. I decided to wait before telling the children. The
next morning I found a single egg, which I did show them,
issuing bloodcurdling threats to prevent their playing
anywhere near the nest or looking at it more than once a day.
The morning after we discovered a second egg, and so it
went on for the next three mornings until a clutch of five had
been laid.

By now we knew the nest was the work of a pair of

chaffinches. We never saw either of them on the nest, but every time we opened the front door we saw a tell-tale flash of white on the wings of a small brown bird which darted from the chestnut across the lawn to hide in a hedge. Our books confirmed that the size and colour of the eggs, as well as the construction of the nest, were those of chaffinches. The eggs were small, no more than three-quarters of an inch high and half an inch wide, and in colour they were a pale greenish-blue, marked with spots and blotches that reminded me of foxing on book pages, only darker stained, and connected with streaks and crack-shaped lines. The nest was moulded to the shape of the corbel or ledge on the side of the trunk which the birds had used as their foundation, but the cup itself was a perfect hollow half-sphere. Its walls were woven laterally out of filaments of dried grass, which were plugged and thickened with moss, the whole thing forming a dense, flexible, wind-proof cushion. At its base the nest was matted round the stems of half a dozen shooting leaves, which acted as joists. The moss had been kept green by the nearly incessant rain we had all endured that month. Evidently, both birds gather the material, but the hen alone does the actual building, often lining the cup with hair and wool, and felting the walls with spiders' web. In this case, the cup was lined with grass and a few downy feathers; it was very soft to the touch.

For a fortnight we inspected the clutch night and morning, the children, as far as I know, sticking obediently to this regimen. The eggs must have been very close to hatching when, one Sunday morning, as we were getting up, my eye was caught by a flicker of colour on the chestnut trunk below. There, at first to our delight, was a woodpecker, unmistakeably hammering its beak against the bark. I knew it to be a great spotted woodpecker from its pied markings and the scarlet patch on the back of its head, which I had looked up only a few days before having seen one drumming in the woods. With quick, jerking movements, it skipped across the face of the trunk, pausing to knock in a nail or two, then jumping back. The chaffinches flew round it in the most agitated way. As it approached the nest, they began to attack it with little fluttering jabs, which the bigger bird easily shook off. I threw open the window, shouting and clapping my hands, only to find the children doing the same from another window, at the risk of their own lives. The woodpecker flew off, and the chaffinch hen returned to her nest. But, ten minutes later, the woodpecker was back, and this time, despite the desperate lunges of the chaffinches, it made directly for the nest. I shouted again from the window, but it took no notice, and we could see the spike of its head banging up and down on the eggs. I had to go downstairs and rush towards the tree, waving my arms and yelling, before I could drive it away.

The fabric of the walls had been badly torn and the whole nest dislodged from its foundation by the fury of the woodpecker's assault, but I was relieved to find that two eggs had survived. However, the chaffinches did not return, and when I looked again I realized that one of the remaining eggs was in fact broken. The other seemed stuck to the bottom of the cup. I tried to roll it over and it proved to be quite hollow, except for a little scrap of shrivelled yoke sac. We could find no trace of broken shell in the nest or on the ground below, and had to conclude that the woodpecker had eaten the eggs whole. It certainly must have considered them a great delicacy to have come so close to the house, something we had never seen before.

That Sunday was quite overcast by the memory of this shocking event. The children did not cry, as they had done, inconsolably, over the death of their jerbil, but they were nevertheless horrified by the wantonness, the sheer barbarity of the woodpecker's attack. It had, after all, committed the foulest of crimes by invading a family, smashing its home and killing – eating – its offspring. This was an atrocity, even under the law of the jungle; for woodpeckers do not rely on a diet of birds' eggs for their survival. It is true that children feel a powerful sense of identification with the fate of all 'baby' creatures, from tadpoles upwards, and will go to enormous and often quite inappropriate lengths to keep them alive, but there was more than infantile self-projection at work on this occasion. We were all appalled and distressed.

Human beings, adults and children alike, have always been able to identify with birds, perhaps more easily than with other animals. Of all the many conservation pressure groups in Europe, the Royal Society for the Protection of Birds is the largest, with a membership of over 340,000 (in 1984), and a junior branch of 110,000 members. The laws protecting birds are far stricter than those relating to other creatures, and are based on a unique principle: all British birds, together with their nests and eggs, are protected from killing, injury and theft, except in certain very clearly defined circumstances. The strength of our concern for birds may be gauged by the fact that these laws do not respect the usual privileges of land ownership. You do not have the right to do as you like with birdlife on your own land; indeed, since 1963, it has been an offence to take so much as a blackbird's egg from a nest in your own garden. Richard Mabey has astutely pointed out that the relative stringency of bird laws owes much to the efforts of pioneer pressure groups, such as the Fur, Fin and Feather Folk, a ladies' tea club in Croydon and ancestor of the present Royal Society for the Protection of Birds, who campaigned to curb the brutal treatment then inflicted on birds. 'Bird protection,' he writes, 'was as much concerned with the quality of human behaviour as the quantity of birds . . .'[1]

Why should birds receive this exceptional attention? On the face of it, they look less anthropomorphically desirable than other species, especially other mammals, for they have feathers, wings, beaks and claws, they are egg-bearing, and they have their existence in a different element, which completely separates them from us. But perhaps their very independence makes their community appear to us like another society, distinct but homologous to our own. The similarities are persuasive: birds bond in pairs, sometimes for life; they build nests in which they produce and nurture their offspring; they have an active family life and educate their young; their occupation of territory is conspicuous; their calls and songs are irresistibly reminiscent of language; and certain species congregate in huge numbers, under crowded conditions, engaging in a complex and harmonious social life, which seems a positive model of city dwelling. They also indulge in activities that have been called proto-aesthetic, that is activities which are, in some rudimentary way, the expression of emotions, or which suggest an enjoyment of decoration for its own sake. Above all, they are highly visible. Because their ability to fly protects them from most predators, they do not behave, as do many other small animals, furtively, avoiding notice. As Claude Lévi-Strauss observed, 'everything objective conspires to make us think of the bird world as a metaphorical human society: is it not after all literally parallel to it on another level?'[2]

But we should not sentimentalize our relationships with birds, which, while extremely close, have also been extremely bloody, exemplifying Wilde's line, 'And all men kill the thing they love'. The need for protective legislation has of course only been prompted by outbreaks of exceptional maltreatment. The first Acts to provide birds with minimal protection during their breeding seasons were passed during the second half of the nineteenth century (in 1869, 1872,

1876 and 1880), a period when sport and the hat trade were between them destroying countless millions of birds.[3] This was the age of the big bag. Until around 1840 game birds had been 'walked up' with dogs, but thereafter it became the fashion to drive them over the guns, which made for a far higher killing rate and called for much less effort and skill. The scale of slaughter was further magnified by the invention of the breech loader and later the double barrel. By 1888, Lord Walsingham was able to kill 1,070 grouse in 14 hours and 18 minutes, using 1,510 cartridges. In 1913, at a battue organized in his honour, George V took part in what was to prove the biggest shoot in history, when 4,000 pheasant were shot, more than a thousand by the royal gun. (Though it was his favourite sport, even he felt rueful after this carnage. 'Perhaps we went a little too far today, David,' he said to his son.) For the commoner sportsman, pigeons released from traps provided the victims; these too were shot in vast numbers. Pigeon shooting, however, was a blood sport that required still less effort and field craft than pheasant shooting, and in the 1870s it began to get a very bad press. But, despite the efforts of the RSPCA and the influence of Princess Alexandra, it was not successfully legislated against until 1921.

Two decades of campaigning against the use of plumage on hats and dresses did nothing to halt demand, which reached its climax in the 1890s. It was calculated that 300 million dead birds were imported by Europe each year, and of them 25 million were brought to England alone. The most notorious dress of the period was trimmed with the feathers of 800 canaries. Nor was the fashion confined to the rich; servants could afford to adorn themselves with the feathers of kingfishers, orioles and birds of paradise. The barred wings of young kittiwakes were much sought after, and some sections of public opinion were sickened by descriptions of traders who shot down the young birds on Lundy Island, tore off their wings, often before they were dead, and flung the dismembered bodies into the sea which ran pink with their blood. But, in the end, it seems to have been the caprice of fashion, rather than humanitarian conscience, that saved the world's bird population from extermination.

At all events, when the next wave of destruction was inflicted on birds in the post-war period as a result of intensified farming methods, no serious resistance was offered by either public opinion or Parliamentary reactionism to the Acts of 1954 and 1967, which secured universal protection for birds, both native and migratory. We are now a reformed nation and look with horror on the behaviour of our Continental neighbours, especially the French and Italians, who continue to slaughter small birds on a scale that we must, in honesty, call Victorian. Naturally, we feel most incensed at the indiscriminate killing of those birds making their way to our shores to breed. What has brought about this reformation of our national character, I cannot say, but the fact is that having been the most reckless slayers of birds we have become the most fastidious of protectors.

It is a fact often remarked on, though nonetheless peculiar, that the thirst to kill animals frequently co-exists with an equally fanatical interest in natural history. Ernest Hemingway provides a famous modern example of this ambivalence, but Charles Darwin provides a more sympathetic one. As a boy, Darwin had a well-developed taste for natural history, and more especially for collecting. Later, towards the end of his schooldays, he developed another taste, which by no means cancelled out the first. 'I became passionately fond of shooting,' he wrote in his autobiography. 'I do not believe that anyone could have shown more zeal for the most holy cause than I did for shooting birds.'

He recorded that the excitement caused by killing his first snipe was so great he could hardly reload his gun for the trembling of his hands. During the same period, however, he read Gilbert White's *Selbourne* and was inspired to make a special study of birds and their habits. 'In my simplicity, I remember wondering why every gentleman did not become an ornithologist.' After school, he was sent to Edinburgh University to study medicine, but he found he was too squeamish to watch surgeons at work in the operating theatre. Instead, he concentrated on his interest in the natural sciences and attended lectures on all sorts of subjects; he remembered hearing Audubon speak about North American birds. Meanwhile, this same gentleman continued to shoot with all his old zeal. His obsession was so compulsive he used to place his shooting boots open by his bed-side to avoid losing the half minute it took to put them on in the morning. Characteristically, he kept an exact record of every bird he shot throughout a season, but he was, of course, too sensitive not to feel the need of some rationalization of his passion. 'I think I must have been half-consciously ashamed of my zeal, for I tried to persuade myself that shooting was almost an intellectual employment; it required so much skill to judge where to find most game and to hunt the dogs well.' In time, however, maturity had its effect and, during his voyage on the *Beagle*, he gradually abandoned shooting in favour of observing. Finally, he gave his gun to his servant. But it is interesting to note that the reason he gave for this change had nothing to do with becoming more humane. He stopped because 'shooting interfered with my work', and he discovered, 'though unconsciously and insensibly, that the pleasure of observing and reasoning was a much higher one than that of skill and sport'.

There can be no doubt that Darwin was in fact a most

humane man, whose scientific approach to his animal subjects was always coloured by sensitivity and a sympathetic humour. Nonetheless, his youthful confessions demonstrate in the most vivid way the potentiality for good and evil, creativity and destructiveness which appears to be an essential element in the human make-up, and part of every individual's endowment. This combination of god and beast, killer and poet, scientist and sadist is at its most ambiguous in our dealings with the natural world. No doubt this is part of our evolutionary heritage as hunter-farmers. But, in the modern period, when most people do not depend on hunting or farming for their livelihood, our attempts to re-engage with nature have taken some brutal forms. The Victorian's mania for collecting was scarcely less destructive than their addiction to shooting for pleasure (sport). Our present good behaviour as protectors of wildlife should not blind us to the fact that we too are heirs to the same congenital schizophrenia. At present, our 'zeal' for killing other living creatures seems to be dominated by the naturalist in us, but this only means we must redouble our efforts to halt those forms of institutional killing which are too casually licensed. These include vivisection and other experiments on live animals, or the destruction of habitats for the sake of lucrative food production, which claims false justification on economic grounds.

To return to our theme: if we are not, with respect to birds, the most knowledgeable generation that has ever lived, we ought to be. Throughout history birds have attracted far more attention from writers and painters (though not from carvers and the makers of other kinds of ornamental patterns, who have preferred fruit and flowers), and compared with the rich and extensive literature devoted to birds, the literature of wild flowers is paltry. In our time, there has been no slackening in the flow of books about birds; indeed, if anything, there has been an increase. As the astonishing membership figures of the RSPB testify, the entire bird population is now being exhaustively studied both at home and in the field by enormous numbers of people. But, as we saw in an earlier chapter, the acquisition of knowledge involves its own kind of loss.

Peggy Munsterberg, editor of the excellent Penguin anthology of bird poetry, makes the point that, while the long-standing folkloric tradition of bird rhymes has been doomed by the spread of industrial society, the decay of the literary bird poem, and for that matter of 'nature' poetry in general, has been mainly caused by the advance of modern science. Bird poetry of the Romantic period reflects a new accuracy in its knowledge of bird behaviour, but despite this realism the choice of birds and their poetic roles tend to be quite conventional. Keats was content to use the nightingale, which by his time was an archetypal poetic figure, because by infusing the many classical and folkloric associations attached to the bird with his own deeply personal response he was able to refresh and rework a familiar, shared tradition. During the nineteenth century, natural history became, for the first time, the business of prose writers. Charles Darwin's grandfather, Erasmus, wrote his discussion of the Linnean system in heroic couplets, and for most people in the eighteenth century James Thomson's long poem *The Seasons* (1730) was their chief source of information concerning zoology, botany and geology. With the rise of popular scientific writing about birds, Victorian poets wrote less and less descriptive verse, and while they developed a Pre-Raphaelite attention to realistic detail, they also began to explore an increasingly personal symbolism. The traditional roles attributed to birds were forgotten in the move from country to town, and were anyway nullified by new scientific understanding. As a result, poets were

THE POETRY OF BIRDS

more or less forced to create private meanings to replace the old, outmoded public ones. Most devastating to all forms of established nature symbolism was the collapse of a credible religious explanation for the creation and existence of 'the animal kingdom'. Some poets, such as Gerard Manley Hopkins, through sheer force of imagination, succeeded in breathing new religious life into old symbols. But most resorted to making a private, secular world of meaning out of their own experience and sensibility. Though far less bird poetry as such is being written today, the situation is much the same. Summing it up, Peggy Munsterberg writes,

> With no generally accepted traditions and no single, readily comprehensible view of nature, poets are at once more isolated and more private than they were in earlier periods, and yet as far as their bird poetry is concerned, it does not represent a radical departure so much as an intensification of Victorian individualism.[4]

We can see the truth of her remark illustrated in Ted Hughes's poem, *The Hawk in the Rain*, published in 1957:

I drown in the drumming ploughland, I drag up
Heel after heel from the swallowing of the earth's mouth,
From clay that clutches my each step to the ankle
With the habit of the dogged grave, but the hawk

Effortlessly at height hangs his still eye.
His wings hold all creation in a weightless quiet,
Steady as a hallucination in the streaming air.
While banging wind kills these stubborn hedges,

Thumbs my eyes, throws my breath, tackles my heart,
And rain hacks my head to the bone, the hawk hangs
The diamond point of will that polestars
The sea drowner's endurance: and I,

Bloodily grabbed dazed last-moment-counting
Morsel in the earth's mouth, strain towards the master-
Fulcrum of violence where the hawk hangs still.
That maybe in his own time meets the weather

Coming the wrong way, suffers the air, hurled upside
    down,
Fall from his eye, the ponderous shires crash on him,
The horizon traps him; the round angelic eye
Smashed, mix his heart's blood with the mire of the land.

For the duration of the poem we can see the hawk through Hughes's eyes; we can feel the drag of our base, earthbound nature as the mud sucks at our boots, and we can feel the airy liberty of the hawk poised above us on a point of wind; through his words, we can also feel the rage of the gale as it hurls the hawk to the ground, returning it to our own dull element. And yet, for all that, the bird remains his invention, his private hallucination, and will not translate itself into public property. It is first Hughes's hawk, then a literary hawk, and only thirdly a hawk in nature. This is not Hughes's fault. It is not a failing in his poem, which is superb; it is the result of our not possessing a common pool of natural symbolism. Such symbolism as we do share consists of the debased tokens used in advertising, where the last croaks of an old and rich vocabulary can still be heard. Lacking Hughes's eloquence and power of vision, we have no choice, once we put down his poem, but to return to the hawk of the guide books, the ornithological hawk, which is a lesser creature, in that it cannot accumulate non-scientific meanings. The poem may well linger affectingly in our mind, and may well be remembered when looking at a real hawk in the sky, but bird and poem now belong to separate cultural categories and no poet, however inspired or however intense his personal vision, can by himself reunite them. In the past, poets were able to draw on and enhance an already existing body of response to a particular bird, and in this way they contributed to, without having to make, the structure of feeling in which they wrote. Today's poet, however, must first provide his own landscape and bestiary, and even then can only sing a solitary song to celebrate or curse his own creation.

But, although nature poetry, like the entire pastoral convention, is withering on the branch, I still believe that a *poetic* response, using that word in its widest application, offers us the means of bridging the separation between ourselves and nature, which I have been trying to describe throughout this book. In the case of birds, our increased knowledge of their ethology and ecology can only assist our poetic enterprise, because owing to our close affinity with birds, we can never treat them with strict ornithological objectivity. All of us can benefit from the rich relationship that continues to exist between birds and even the most enclosed city dweller. Scientific perceptions of nature, together with the whole tendency of our industrial society, have certainly put paid to the old vernacular and rural mythologies attached to birds, and they cannot be revived as living traditions, though they should not be forgotten and lost. Yet, such is the strength of our identification with birds that, far from killing or obstructing it, our new knowledge of their habits can only reinforce the bond.

I am not discussing anything that is not already happening. To attempt to prescribe people's feelings would be futile, and I am only putting words to an experience that is commonplace. However, I do think it is helpful to stress that, though many of the traditional ties that bound us to the bird community have rotted and broken, we still have our purely sensuous appreciation of birds, which combined with our ecological awareness, makes us more than capable of replacing the old symbolism with a new aesthetic. But this modern sensibility calls for an unabashed confidence in our 'poetic' powers.

To a non-European eye, used to the exotic plumage of the tropics, our British bird life must at first glance seem drab, the overwhelming impression being of small, brown creatures who are shy and difficult to observe. But, like much natural beauty in Britain, our birds are wonderfully rewarding to eyes that are adapted to enjoy subtle, delicate effects. The slick green sheen of an adult starling glistening in a cool October sun; the chestnut breast and slate-blue head of a male chaffinch; the black head of a bullfinch and its glowing salmon-pink breast; the grey-suited and white-collared respectability of the woodpigeon made suspect by its flashy green neckerchief; the blue tit's pastel colours daubed together from a child's palette; these are ordinary beauties, to be found in any country garden, but they nonetheless give great pleasure. We have our exotics as well. No one who has seen a kingfisher tear a turquoise slit in a pure blue sky as it streaks into hiding from its spearing perch on a willow branch, will ever forget its irrisdescence. Unforgettable too is the sight of the first spring goldfinch pairs, back from their Continental winter and quite ornamental enough to hold their own in the lushest jungle. And the jay, a despised bird, enemy of gamekeeper and gardener alike, lolloping in the air despite its look of strength, carries on its wings feathers which are tinted the most vivid cobalt, the effect heightened by bars of jet black. I once found one of these dazzling feathers lying among some ferns in our wood, and at first took it for a piece of mislaid jewelry, a sapphire brooch or bracelet. I kept it in my room for a year, and it never lost its brilliance.

Wild flowers do not last long, and they last no longer for the rich. In the same way, owning a large, secluded garden, full of rare plants, is no guarantee in itself that rare birds will take up residence; nor does it guarantee the presence of some common ones, like the robin, for example, which prefers the back yard and the kitchen garden. Gardens are of course also inhabited by mammal life, and as many surveys have shown, even town gardens turn out to be surprisingly well-populated. However, on the few occasions when one sees a fox, say, or a stoat, it is likely to be at twilight, and the animal is likely to be scurrying apprehensively out of sight. (In the ten years I have lived here in Suffolk, I have only once come across a hedgehog. One evening, walking round the garden, I heard a loud coughing noise, a sort of rasping, bronchial grunt, and there at my feet quite unaware of my presence was a large hedgehog. It lumbered past me at a brisk pace, almost bumping into my shoes, and disappeared into the darkness, still heartily clearing its throat.) Birds, however, having much less to fear from humans, are more often at their ease, and can be seen openly going about their business. As I type this, I can see a family of robins sunning themselves beneath a thorn hedge where they have their nest. The parents are casually on guard while their two fat, speckled fledglings, who as yet have no trace of red on their breasts, are making inexpert dives from a low branch into the grass.

The most fearless and foolish birds we have in our garden are pheasants. Hand-fed, pampered and protected, the foppish cocks strut about the estate in fatuous arrogance, and like members of some decadent *ancien régime*, have no inkling of their inevitable end. More cautious are the wild red-legged partridges, which during the winter months keep mostly to the hedges and open ploughed fields where their camouflage protects them well. To us in the house, however, they are very noticeable because of their extreme vociferousness. Walking indian-file in a small gang, they have often woken us early in the morning with their harsh 'chaka chaka chaka' cries, which they repeat incessantly and, to our aggrieved ears, pointlessly, since the sound seems to be neither musical nor communicative.

In the early summer, most garden and woodland birds, having young to feed and nurture, are of course especially conspicuous. Last week, a family of young blackbirds, fresh out of their nest, plump and spoilt, made an irresistibly comic sight as they teetered to and fro on a beam in our garage. Too frightened to launch into the wind, too hungry to delay, and too big to return to the security of the nest, they lurched and fluttered for a whole morning in an agony of indecision, until at last they gained their gangling wings or simply fell off and found themselves launched.

Whereas wild flowers can be picked, brought home and studied in detail, without having their essential qualities destroyed, birds must be left alive in their element. Eggs and nests can be collected and examined, and fledglings which have fallen out of the nest can sometimes be successfully fed and rescued, but for the most part birds, though so close at hand, can only be observed from a respectful distance. Yet it is just this paradoxical combination of closeness and independence that makes them so significant to us. Their essence is always intact, and seems magically superior to ours, which, like that of other mammals, is never free from the threat of some terrestrial indignity. Their careless mastery of the air makes them a primary symbol of transcendence over the daily cares and squalors from which those of us who trudge the face of the earth are seldom released. Ever since the Romantic period, when our sense of being displaced in existence, of self-alienation, was first most keenly felt and voiced, birds have seemed to fly not just in the air, but in the ether of liberty. Even the tattiest sparrow, the most bedraggled pigeon, has the power to fly above its situation and escape the intolerable here and now. Birds even seem immune from the law of mortality, the thought of which, if not the fact, is never out of our calculations. Flowers, like flesh, visibly corrupt and decay on the stalk, but though the odd body of a dead bird may be found, the species prevails eternally (or rather for as long as we refrain from putting it into extinction). Birds, and especially those, such as the swallow, lark, nightingale, eagle, or owl, which appear to us to possess extraordinary powers, are perceived as an ideal, an image of our aspirations. And yet birds are also bound by the same constrictions as us, by their sexual and family life, and by their need to protect and provide. More perhaps than any other branch of nature, bird life strikes us as a realization of our own possibilities: we can see in the achievements of birds a metaphor, which, if resolved into human terms, would transfigure our being.

The idea is not to rescue birds for poetry, but to rescue ourselves through our poetic perceptions. I do not believe in the perfectability of Man, nor do I believe, though I count myself a socialist, in the possibility of an ideal political system capable of liberating us from conditions which, allegedly, force us at present to behave in a way that is contrary to our true natures. We are not so much flawed as divided; the evil potentiality within us must be forcibly repressed, not merely by laws, but by a self-imposed morality conceived in the full knowledge of our destructive, cruel and bloody side. But the creative, loving side of our being needs its own help and sustenance. In the absence of traditional forms of idealism and moral discipline, which are provided by communal religions deriving from belief in a superhuman authority, we must devise a humanistic ethic. For, paradoxically, we will never contain the evil in us unless we can hold up that portrait of ourselves which was best expressed by Shakespeare:

What a piece of work is a man, how noble in reason, how
infinite in faculties, in form and moving how express and
admirable, in action how like an angel, in apprehension
how like a god . . .

(Hamlet, II.2.303)

Such a notion of our sublime capability must in the end be
built on self-belief, but it can nevertheless draw inspiration
from seeing an image of our transfigured selves shaped out in
the power and beauty of natural life. And, in this respect,
birds do indeed represent a poetic ideal.

MEMORY AND IMAGINATION

———————————————

To a small child, there is no such thing as landscape. His mind does not deal readily in generalities and abstractions, and his world is made up of the singular and unique. His eye grasps only one thing at a time and has no facility for unifying bits of land and sky into the single sweep that is landscape. His vision is fragmented, focusing on parts, not wholes. William Hazlitt wrote in the opening lines of his famous essay,

> Distant objects please because, in the first place, they imply an idea of space and magnitude, and because, not being obtruded too close upon the eye, we clothe them with the indistinct and airy colours of fancy.

But distant objects do not seem to please children; if anything, they seem to disturb them. Space and magnitude, far from liberating the child's mind as they do the adult's, are elements in which the child drowns, his scarcely formed identity shredding in the void. Mostly, however, children ignore the sublime. Sunsets do not move them; nor do the soaring heights of cathedral architecture. Such beauties have to be pointed out to them and are only acknowledged with politeness.

Much as it grieves the cultivated middle-class parent such as myself to admit it, in matters of taste children show an incorrigible preference for the gaudy and meretricious. No amount of worthy-minded exposure to good and beautiful things will reform their love of plastic over wood, trash over quality, vulgarity over refinement. The home-made, hand-painted, authentically-scaled wooden doll's house does not stand a chance beside its over-priced, mass-produced, instantly collapsible plastic equivalent. But to talk of children, at least small children, exercising taste is almost meaningless. They do not apply judgement; instead, they are irresistibly attracted to bright colours and things that easily lend themselves to being stroked, manipulated and generally played with, things in fact which 'obtrude close upon the eye'. And, of course, they respond to small objects and miniatures of every kind, from dolls to toy cars to lambs. It is not philistinism that makes them indifferent to the splendour of Ely's Octagon and Lantern tower; they simply cannot accommodate anything on that scale, however beautiful to the adult eye. By the same token, the aesthetic appeal of gardens tends to leave them cold, though they are excited by individual flowers and, unless restrained, will gleefully pick the place bare.

For most children, place is part of the given world in which they find themselves, and their perception of it is myopic, patchy and unquestioning. The way they inhere in their surroundings, their house and garden, their furniture, toys and clothes, is closer to that of animals than adults. They have no understanding of the arbitrary, accidental pattern of events that led to their being in one place rather than another, just as an infant takes some time to distinguish between himself and his mother's breast, to accept his autonomy with all its hazards and frustrations, so children only gradually learn they exist separately from family and home.

From the garden of my own boyhood I remember a laburnum tree which stood in what seemed to me a far-off province of our small back lawn. I was fascinated by its long dangling chains of yellow flowers and also by the deadly properties I was taught to believe its blackened seed pods possessed. I remember too the mature lime which grew in a murky patch of shrubbery at the front of our house and which helped to form a dank bower for our garage. This was a truly suburban tree. Its magnificent, luminescent canopy was supported by a scruffy trunk that was crammed into the angle between a privet hedge and a brick wall. Nor was it left to enjoy the exclusive use of its wretched corner, which served the pavement as a casual refuse bin, filling up with lolly wrappers in summer and its own rotting leaves in winter. However, it had its revenge by dripping midsummer gum on to the roof of our car.

These trees were just two pieces of the stage set in which my childhood was acted out. To me, as a small child, they were no different in essence to the greenhouse, the coal bunkers, the gallows-like swing my father put up for me, or the stone frog which crouched on our crazy paving. It was some years before I saw them as trees living out an independent existence, and stopped thinking of them as parts of our garden, as facilities to be played on or shapes painted on a backdrop. And it was still more years before I fully realized that these same species were to be seen in most gardens up and down the road. They were not, after all, as I had unconsciously assumed, single specimens particular to our family garden.

An even greater shock came with the discovery that the beach near my grandfather's farm in South Wales – Broadhaven, a classic formation of dunes, cliffs, caves, rocks and pools, and a huge acreage of pale, fine sand – was not the only one of its kind. I still think there is no other beach to touch it for both beauty and sheer amusement, but I was shocked to find out that there were other beaches at all, that moreover they were a commonplace feature of coasts all round the country and therefore not a peculiarity of the Home Farm, Stackpole, where I was born.

Such realizations are, of course, much more emotional than rational and tend to be delayed until long after the objective facts have been absorbed. Knowledge has to be felt as well as known before it makes any real impact. Also, a natural snobbery in favour of the superiority of one's own experience plays its part here and retards our awareness of the boring fact that we are, by and large, more like than unlike our fellow men and women. But even after the broader, realistic perspective has been admitted, the old associations still linger, giving words and places primary meanings that are not to be found in dictionaries and gazeteers. The word *beach* is forever Broadhaven to me, and only thereafter does it signify other, ordinary beaches.

John Constable, writing of the Stour valley where he had lived as a boy and where, as a painter, he returned every summer to sketch and pursue his sad, interminable courtship of Maria Bicknell, declared, 'these scenes made me a painter'. It is often thought extraordinary that his famous landscapes of Dedham, Flatford and East Bergholt, pictures which have since come to stand as the acme of pastoral Romanticism, were in fact painted from notes and memory in his London studio. The pictures themselves certainly are extraordinary, as was the man's tenacity in the face of poverty and neglect, but his ability to carry back to town the landscape of his boyhood, intact and vital, is perhaps not so remarkable. Admittedly, his celebrated notebooks did provide him with an almost comprehensive portrait in miniature of the Stour valley and its farms; however, he could also draw on that fertile resource of self-refreshing memory, which appears to be the special property of those who remain faithful to one place from childhood onwards.

No great act of recall was required to recreate a landscape he had by then converted into the very fibre of his mind. His sketches served to remind him of indispensable visual details, but it was the preservation of his original response to these 'scenes' that gave the pictures their unique emotional tone.

It is no co-incidence that many of his 'six footers', the big canvasses he prepared during the winter months for the annual Academy exhibition in May, contain figures of children, for it is a childhood vision of the Suffolk countryside that he recaptures. Constable is often accused of being as much of a reactionary in his painting as he undoubtedly was in his politics. But I would suggest that his conservatism does not lie in his editing out of the landscape those labourers whose gruelling, wretchedly paid work was responsible for much of its beauty, nor in coating the countryside with a golden glow of harmony which was false when he was painting in the 1820s and was scorched off for good in the rick-burning riots of 1830. His conservatism was more dynamic than that. Everything in his best pictures is heightened, emotionally and visually. That famous dewy freshness recalls the intoxication and innocence of childhood's first outdoor adventures. To this degree his conservatism was radical, for it offered a view of reality transformed by feeling, though securely footed in observation. But its strength is also its weakness because, being a vision derived from childhood, it is changeless or, rather, static. 'I even love every stile and stump, and every lane in the village,' he confessed, 'so deeply rooted are early impressions'. And it is this deep-rootedness in his own past which gives the pictures a personal, more than political, conservatism: the vibrancy, for all its magical intensity, will go on forever, never yielding to anything new.

Ronald Blythe, who has himself lived and worked most of

his life in a part of Suffolk very close to Constable's, writes of having two states of landscape consciousness: 'The first I would call instinctive and unlettered, a mindfulness of my own territory which has been artlessly and sensuously imbibed.' The second, he says, is the product of adult knowledge about the same countryside drawn from science, sociology, art and religion. But they are not easily reconciled; there is a dilemma of intuition versus tuition:

> I find myself constantly hankering after primordial statements which still float around in my memory, and which seem to say something more relevant about my own geography than anything my trained intelligence can tell me, yet which tantalisingly avoids definition.[1]

This is very well put. It was part of Constable's genius not only to reconcile these two states of consciousness but to fuse them in a single, highly productive creativity. Borrowing Blythe's words, one might describe Constable's art as trained primordialism.

However, the dilemma Blythe speaks of is something of a specialist one, which faces those few people who grow up to live and work in the locality of their childhood. Most people do not show the same fixedness: they leave home in search of a job, and most find themselves in a city. But whether they originally come from a town or country background, the transition from school to work, from childhood to adulthood, involves some impoverishment of their sensuous life as they move into the bleaker, harder, more confining environment of factory or office. For a few, professional rewards and satisfactions will compensate for this deprivation, but for the majority going to work for the first time will be marked by a sense of loss, a feeling that the prison-house door has closed on them. (One of the many cruelties of the present situation of unemployment is that those school leavers who do find work are bound to feel relief, not regret, at the extinction of their 'fair and shining youth'.)

Once at work, their sense of place becomes blunted. The singularities of childhood, so vividly caught in Constable's pocket-book sketches, dissolve into generalities, and finally expire in a mist of nostalgia. Their primordial intimacy with the physical world withers, reviving fitfully on visits 'home' and on holidays to the seaside or ski slopes, but dying in the end. Meanwhile, that second state of landscape consciousness defined by Ronald Blythe, which emanates from the 'trained intelligence', fails to develop.

Of course, it is true that merely to survive in our increasingly ugly and inhospitable world we are bound to let our sensitivity to place grow a little numb; madness or monasticism are the only alternatives. But, tragically, for all too many people the places where they live and work give no pleasure or excitement – as places – but must instead be endured, or ignored. This loss of our infantile delight in place is, I believe, a severe handicap, which has somehow to be repaired if we are to bring our feelings for nature back to life. We have to learn once more to love every stile and stump, and every land in whichever 'village' we find ourselves.

Last summer, I used to take my children to a farmyard where they learned to ride their bicycles. Watching them weave and wobble among the dried tractor ruts, I was always drawn to a broken-down fuel tank on wheels, which had collapsed against a wall of the farrowing house. Its tyres were irreparably flat, and the earth and weeds below its spigot were thickly soaked in diesel oil. On a hot evening, when this little slick was still glitteringly fluid, its pungent fumes would mix with the smell of pig dung and harvest dust, and together they used to have an almost convulsive impact on my memory. I was instantaneously returned to my own early childhood.

Most people, I suppose, have in their past a golden age, or at least a period which conjures up especially good memories. My own golden age is not the product of a specific year; nor are all its associations by any means happy ones. As a small boy, I used to be taken by my parents for holidays to my grandfather's farm, and, like all family holidays, ours were not entirely free of tension and conflict, of which I was, no doubt, as much the cause as the victim. But I do remember with deep satisfaction playing on my own in the cowsheds, barns and yard, which had been so vividly evoked by the tang of diesel oil. Here, sunk in a kind of trance, I would amuse myself hour after hour: I drove motionless tractors at breakneck speed, skipped stones across the dusty potholes, and heroically saved my family from attacks of marauding enemies.

Thus, my evocative oil recalled a mood of childhood, rather than a chain of suddenly rediscovered incidents. This mood was not linked to any one holiday or occasion; instead, it represented the essence of all those farmyard games, distilled into a single, very poignant sensation.

These pangs of memory are, of course, not confined to rural incidents. I experience similar feelings at the sight of rusting chains, slimy hawsers, capstans, bollards and all the other paraphernalia of a dockside. As an adolescent, together with countless other Liverpudlians, I was very fond of walking down Water Street to the Pier Head and on to the old floating landing stage, now alas dismantled. Hardly a week passed without my taking the ferry over the river to Birkenhead to look back across the dirty, dramatic Mersey at the doomed pomp of Liverpool's waterfront façade. Back on the city side, I used to lean over the railings and stare down at the black water swilling over the massive links that helped to bind the floating pier to its bank. Whenever I see quayside chains nowadays, I am reminded of those trips on the river. Predictably, my recollection of them has been condensed into one perfect trip, and in its turn this has come to stand as an emotive token of my Liverpool youth, or at least its happier aspects.

In order to crystallize the past in this way, the mind first has to select, distort and compress its subject matter before producing what is in effect a single, highly-charged memory myth. Clearly, these memory myths will not stand examination in the light of strict biographical truth, but that does not mean they deserve to be dismissed as self-indulgent fancies. They do bear a relationship to this truth, albeit an oblique one, and they also possess a truth of their own, a metaphorical truth to which biographical and historiographic criteria do not apply. They are metaphors invented to digest and make sense of the past; they provide a way of giving significant shape to the sequence of events that make up the development of self. They are necessary legends, without which our past experience would be nothing but a chaos of footprints in the mud. We are creatures of time no less than place, and we cannot proceed lucidly through time unless we first devise an intelligible account of the history that brought us to the present. This is as true of the individual as it is of society, and for both, the process of understanding their origins in time involves a measure of unavoidable, indeed indispensable, myth-making. Myths are the poetic expression of experience; they owe their truth to lived events, but cannot be deconstructed into them.

The minds of small children are resolutely focused on the present and the immediate future. All experience is exceptional to them; everything is new and distinct. The past closes up behind them immediately, while the future is a largely unimagined blank. They live on the edge of time. Like animals, they are absorbed in the present, in time being, and make no history of their own. They love to hear their brief lifestory, but it is all legend to them, having no echo in their own memory. Adult notions of the sequence of time and the ordering or cycle of existence have no meaning for them: all meals were 'supper' to my three-year-old son. When asked to make calculations about time, they mouth a language that has no significance and the results are either crazy or comical. According to my son, I was older than his grandfather, my father. They are ferocious protectors of ritual, which is the only calibration of time they grasp. Ritual helps to secure their shallow footing in existence, but each replay is relished as if it were fresh and unprecedented.

What makes children tiring to be with is not so much their energy, which is indeed daunting, as the intensity of their involvement in the here and now. They seem to penetrate the present in a way that adults never do except in dreams or when undergoing extremes of misery and elation, states of mind that are a partial return to childhood. Having eaten of the fruit of knowledge, adults must protect themselves against being thrust so deeply and helplessly into experience. Much of life is only bearable because of our capacity to fantasize about a better situation, or to concentrate on the tolerable sides of an intolerable whole. To be rendered utterly vulnerable, to be deprived of the consolation that pain can pass in time and that the future does hold the chance of change, to be imprisoned in a cell with no windows looking out on memory or hope, to be confined, in short, within the mind of a child would be to suffer as only the most maltreated prisoners do, and to go mad as they must surely do.

On the other hand, one of the joys of having children is being able to participate for a little while in their Zen-like immersion in any activity, especially play. In fact that is what defines play. It is not a special category of game, it is oblivion within it. If children were burdened with a sense of personal history, if they could recall and reconstruct yesterday, they would be quite unable to achieve this total inherence in the present and their ability to go on learning would be shut down. That, presumably, is what happens to severely traumatized children. Having no sense of time, but having been robbed of the childhood gift of forgetfulness, their wound is newly opened each day. They know too much to learn any more.

Small children do apprehend certain, highly selective aspects of the past: apart from enjoying the legend of their own life story and that of their parents, especially those chapters relating to their own origins, they acquire an awareness of history in the shape of 'the olden days'. This, in terms of life, is an entirely flat era, comprising the days of Adam and Eve, dinosaurs, castles and the day before yesterday, with no recognition of relative antiquity. What is striking about the pleasure they take in their own story is that it is heavily treacled over with nostalgia. This gross sentimentality towards themselves as babies is partly a rejoicing in their own comparative maturity, but it is also an expression of pure self-love. Their nostalgia is not a sophisticated emotion, but nor is it a superficial one. In the minds of children, who are fundamentally forward-looking, sentimental narcissism seems to be a function of development whereby they anchor themselves in the swirling confusion of time to a good image of their essential selves. It goes without saying that in this situation concern for the truth is quite irrelevant, for sentimentality is playing a wholly benign and beneficial role. None but the most neurotic or sadistic parent would insist on a child growing up with a fully informed awareness of the irritation he or she had innocently inflicted as a baby by crying, staying awake, rejecting food and so on. Here, nostalgia must be allowed to fulfil its purpose, which turns out to be productive and creative.

With age of course comes an expanding perception of time, though this never becomes a fixed viewpoint; differing phases of maturity bring their own, distinctive fields of vision, culminating in the narrowing focus of the aged on their earliest years. In childhood, the memory seems to act like a one-way valve: it receives its material – indeed, if one believes the assertions of some psychologists, it preserves everything, including impressions unconsciously recorded – but releases very little, leaving the mind free to grow. Later, however, the door begins to swing easily in both directions, permitting both access and discharge, though complicated processes of censorship and reshaping operate on the material as it moves in either direction. Then, in old age, the hinge begins to stiffen and the flow of memory becomes more outward than inward. The great store of recollection now remains permanently unlocked, while the ability to stock up memories of fresh events declines. However, this outpouring of veteran memory cannot be described as nostalgic, for it is not a sentimental indulgence but a reorienting of the mind's energy, which becomes as fixedly backward-looking as a child's is forward-looking and is beyond individual control. Thus senility, if that is the right term for retrospection in the old, offers a means of preparing for death as well as insulating against its imminence.

It is the business of adulthood to strike a balance between past and future, to reconcile experience with expectation, disappointment with ambition. In the process of reckoning up the scope of one's identity, nostalgia, or as I prefer to call it, the making of memory-myths, has a vital part to fill; by the same token, so has the capacity to fantasize about future achievement. No book would ever get written, no garden would be planted out, no love affair would flower into marriage, no creative effort of any kind would ever be attempted if its creator were not first able to dream of feats hitherto unattained and willing to place faith in his or her dreams. Illusions, in a word, are essential to our imaginative wellbeing. Indeed, I would go further and say that illusion is indispensable to conceiving all kinds of models for improvement, whether religious, ethical, political or social; naturally, such models will be derived in part from previous experience, but they will be worthless if they do not dare to aspire beyond the realms of existing capability.

The peculiar process of nostalgia, whereby grief over what has been lost is inseparably mixed with pleasure at remembering it, is in effect a gesture of self-love, or at least of self-acceptance. Furthermore, some measure of healthy nostalgia for childhood, youth and the lost world that made us is a necessary precondition of our ability to fantasize about an unprecedented future. Nostalgia and idealism are the balanced parts of a continuum. At its most fruitful, this re-acceptance of the past encourages the process by which experience of life and self are converted into art. To cut oneself off from childhood, to close down memory, is to be excluded from an extremely fertile stimulus. It is a form of self-mutilation, which ensures only a distorted and diminished use of one's creative powers. On the other hand, to re-incorporate childhood into adult sensibility, as Constable did, is to set free these powers. Thus, nostalgia, if that is still the appropriate word, has a vital contribution to make to the maturing of the imagination.

POSITIVE NOSTALGIA

Nostalgia is of course not confined to individuals; societies are just as prone to the disease. Nothing seems to cause more widespread epidemics of nostalgia than the countryside, and no age seems to have been more susceptible to infection than our own. The eighteenth century had its Pastoral Ideals, and the nineteenth its Rural Revival Movement, but we, by contrast, suffer from chronic Rustic Sentimentality. Or so we are told by the sternest of our country doctors.

As is often the case with social ills, the diagnosis is blunted by a lack of precise terms. Whatever it is we feel about the countryside, it can no longer appropriately be called pastoralism. But that is not because a form of rural idealism no longer exists; it does, and in many respects is similar to traditional pastoralism, though it inspires a very different kind of literature. Modern ruralism, for which a suitable name has yet to be minted, is made up of a complex amalgam of feelings, but when they cannot be lumped under the heading of conservationism, they tend to be condemned as a further outbreak of nostalgia. This is an unjust dismissal of emotions that deserve more respect, and, as it happens, it involves a very partial use of a word which can be interpreted in a positive light.

The word turns out to have a curious history. It was invented in 1678 by a Swiss medical writer, Johannes Hofer, to describe extreme conditions of homesickness, which he did indeed classify as a definite illness. He called it *nostalgie*, deriving this from the Greek words *nostos*, meaning return, and *algos* meaning pain. He reported that the outstanding symptoms of the condition were melancholia, insomnia, anorexia, loss of thirst, palpitations of the heart, smothering sensations, stupor and, of course, persistent thinking about home. He noticed that its victims were more often struck in winter than any other season and this he attributed to the sadness aroused by dead leaves and the cold, hazy sun. Although he recommended purgatives, he stated that the chances of recovery were entirely dependent on whether or not the patient could be returned home.

Following the appearance of Hofer's dissertation in 1685, many articles were published on the subject, most of them by medical men. Soon enough, there was hardly a single mental or physiological disorder that had not been interpreted as nostalgia. Severe attacks were understood to lead to suicide and in 1795, nostalgia and crime were related for the first time when a servant girl who was notoriously homesick set fire to her employer's house. Fire-raising was found to be a common response and many writers believed that when nostalgia affected adolescents it would take one of two forms, melancholia or pyromania. Some victims were driven to psychotic violence, even murder, allegedly deluding themselves that afterwards they would be free to go back home. For many years, the disease was thought to be confined to Switzerland but in 1774 it was reported that thousands of Scottish soldiers had died of homesickness. In time the literature, which turns out to be surprisingly extensive, showed that nostalgia was ubiquitous, having no special bias in terms of race or gender, though uneducated country girls were generally held to be most vulnerable.

Many theories were advanced to account for its existence. Hofer himself explained it as a migration of the animal spirits from the inner brain. Some writers saw it as a form of insanity, while others offered instinct theories. One writer, eschewing psychic explanations, argued that it was the result of increased air pressure, such as mountain people might experience when moving to the lowlands. Young poeple, he maintained, were more susceptible than their elders because their finer-textured skin was less able to withstand the change in pressure. These, and many other antiquated absurdities, continued to be put forward as explanations until as late as our own century. Even Willis H. McCann, the American psychologist writing in 1941 (whose review of the historical literature I have relied on here), discusses nostalgia as if it were a distinct neurosis, which a therapist could isolate and treat.[1]

The word became established in the English language around 1780, but it was not until towards the end of the next century that it ceased to be a specifically clinical term and acquired its wider metaphorical meaning. Oddly enough, however, that august authority, *The Oxford English Dictionary* (1971), restricts its definition of the word to Hofer's original concept of homesickness and makes no mention of the meaning usually attached to it today: 'yearning for what is past or inaccessible; sentimental evocation of past happiness'. *The Penguin English Dictionary* (1969), from which that definition is taken, also adds 'homesickness', but in practice *nostalgia* has virtually shed its first meaning. For example, one would no longer say of a child unhappily languishing at boarding school that he was suffering from nostalgia. Indeed, the word is nowadays used almost entirely in a derogatory sense to describe a sickly attitude to the past, a perversion of historical or biographical truth for the sake of cheap or 'unearned' feelings. (It was James Joyce who once called sentimentality 'unearned emotion'.) And so, in less than 200 years, a word which was

113

coined to give a name to one of the most authentic of emotions has come to define one of the most spurious.

This strange evolution has unfortunately left us without a word to distinguish between the two quite separable nuances of meaning given by the Penguin dictionary, between a sentimental evocation of the past and a genuine yearning for it. This latter 'homesickness' is, however, not easily described because it is a paradoxical emotion, combining grief with consolation. Just as memories of home make the homesick melancholy, but comfort them too, so memories of a personal or historical past can both sadden and cheer at once.

The accusation generally brought against nostalgia is that it knows no history, or rather that its approach to history is wilfully and dishonestly selective. It falsifies by sugaring the past on which it feeds: the boring, painful and dishonourable parts are all ruthlessly forgotten, while the agreeable parts are grossly inflated, even imagined. Following from this is another charge, that nostalgia is at bottom defeatist and thus reactionary. Instead of fabricating dreams of a better future, its response to present evils is to surrender and seek compensation by fleeing to a fallacious past.

Certainly, when we look at the nostalgia surrounding the countryside and its recent past these charges seem amply justified. And yet our feelings are richer and more ambivalent than our account of nostalgia will allow, for they comprise both sentimentality and this other emotion, this amalgam of sorrow and pleasure, for which we have no name. The problem is that these two strains of nostalgia, the authentic and the indulgent, the profound and the superficial, are often inseparably intermingled. Nonetheless, although the old medical writers may have dreamt up explanations for homesickness which look laughable to us, they were surely right to recognize that they were dealing with a very powerful phenomenon.

The memory-myths used by individuals to come to terms with the making of self have their analogies in the collective mind and its idea of our national identity. Raymond Williams has shown us that ever since the rise of urban civilization, each generation has nursed its own version of a rural golden age, a mirage that is usually seen just dipping below the horizon of living memory, while casting a glow over the period co-inciding with the childhood years of the old. Throughout the most recent boom in ruralism and 'country book' publishing, our own nostalgia has been focused on the late Victorian and Edwardian era, the last long hot summer before mechanization and the motor car ruined the countryside. For every book published on the contemporary countryside, two at least must have been published describing the good old days of Edith Holden, Flora Thompson and the rest. And, to prove the accuracy of Williams's observation, nostalgia's dateline is steadily creeping forward. The 1920s, the 1930s (the period, for example, of James Herriot's earliest and best books) and even the war years have acquired the aura, if not of a golden age, at least an age of greater rural charm than our own. Nostalgia has begun to dissolve those grim years into an age to envy.

There are a number of sad ironies attached to the years that fall within our nostalgic perspective. Not the least of them is the fact that the era with which we have been infatuated also happened to contain some of the worst passages of agricultural despression in modern history. The very qualities we have been cherishing and reconstructing – the whole clutch of home-made, handmade, traditionally crafted, scrubbed and unpainted rusticana – were in reality the ingenious, not to say desperate, products of hardship and isolation. Furthermore, this period, from 1875 to 1939, brought to a close the autonomous years of the countryside, for during those years rural industry and society gradually became more and more subordinate not only to urban money and political power, but to urban culture as well. And so nostalgia has, in effect, been celebrating the death throes of rural England's independence, mistaking them for symptoms of the good life.

A blacker irony still is that the same period encompasses the history of modern conservation. It was only in the last two decades of the nineteenth century that large numbers of people responded to the 'pastoral impulse' by suddenly seeing the need to save the countryside from extinction. Their sense of impending loss inspired an impressive display of energy across a large spread of concerns. Within a few years, the foundations of a preservation movement had been laid: the Society for the Protection of Birds, for instance, was launched in 1889, while the National Trust bought its first property in 1895. A host of societies sprang up to save footpaths, commons, ancient buildings and monuments, folk dances and folk songs, 'peasant arts' and so on. Although many of their notions of rural authenticity look arbitrary and quaint to us, the institutions these Victorian pioneers set up and the principles they established are more or less the ones we respect today. It is therefore all the more shocking to realize that this same countryside, which to the late Victorians looked tragically depleted and in desperate need of salvage, now looks desirably rich to us and is the object of countless re-creations in books, films and, above all, in advertisements and television commercials.

We have been so deeply sucked into the vortex of destruction that we have lost all sense of history and nostalgia runs riot. We are being whirled through the gyres of change and deprivation too fast for us to keep our heads and preserve any standards of comparison. Almost any period of the past that seems more stable than our own is enviable to us. Nor, frankly, have we discovered any really effective means of slowing these spirals; we seem able only to accelerate them, and now they threaten to split and burst into chaos. But perhaps the cycle of obliteration will, after all, remain under control as each successive generation accommodates to an every emptier landscape. Perhaps our great-grandchildren in the 2080s will look back on the end of our century and sigh for it as another lost golden age. Perhaps this very book will be dug out by some astute young editor and reprinted as part of a revival of late twentieth century ruralism.

Although the Victorian preservationists were reacting to an objective crisis, which certainly required the kind of remedial action they took, they were nevertheless affected by their own brand of nostalgia. They harked back to an idea of Old England in the age of crafts and small communities that preceded the horrors and inhumanities of industrialism. They were also strongly influenced by the gothic and even the neo-classical idealism of their day. However, what separates them from today's conservationists is that their ambition was not merely to protect the countryside, but to live out a certain country way of life and rehabilitate it for the benefit of the entire rural community. To this end, some people, followers of Ruskin, Carpenter, Kropotkin and Tolstoy, struggled to create a radical agriculture based on communal ownership and co-operative labour. Unfortunately, but inevitably, they failed to survive themselves and in the end were unable to offer the ordinary farm worker anything more inspiring than extreme hard work, with which he was already far too familiar. Others, taking their lead from William Morris, set about researching, recording and rescuing those arts and crafts they deemed historically genuine and worthy of salvation. Many of their efforts now appear rather ludicrous to us, and a few turn out to have been positively damaging, but either way their campaign was largely in vain. They were fighting to breathe life into a culture and an economy that had by then been driven to its deathbed by forces far too powerful to be repulsed by middle-class antiquarians and idealists. But for all that, theirs was a responsible – and impressively knowledgeable – attempt to plant pastoralism in real soil.

In her excellent book on the Victorian pastoralists, Jan Marsh points to the arresting number of priorities shared in common by the older movement and the hippy ruralism of the 1960s and early 1970s.[2] Like their forerunners, yesterday's eco-freaks aspired to self-sufficiency, revived handicrafts and valued a simplification of life style; they also favoured vegetarianism and varieties of eastern mysticism. However, harsher times and a plutocratic agriculture which has no room for the small farmer never mind the communard, have between them closed the lane leading back to the land. A bleaker perception of the planet's fate has also put paid to the idealist optimism of ten years ago, though a strong residue of pastoralism is still to be seen in the campaign against Cruise missiles, the latest and foulest of the countryside's pollutants. The very form of protest adopted by the Greenham women owes something to earlier, 'alternative' communities; indeed, their camp, maintained in defiance of authority's attempts to demolish it, has a direct antecedent in the colony established on St George's Hill by the Diggers at the end of the Civil War. But idealism has become a matter of denying death, rather than planting life.

But the real difference between the two generations of ruralists is that the commune builders of the 1970s were never other than marginal figures pursuing a way of living that was essentially a form of psycho-spiritual therapy. Their beliefs and methods did not amount to a radical

example which the country community at large might have
followed. The modern commune tended to be introverted
and primarily concerned with healing wounds inflicted by a
hostile society outside or seeking some way of self-
development within a closed group. (For a disillusioned, but
understanding account of commune life and its hazards, see
Philip Toynbee's moving diary, *Part of a Journey*, 1981.)
The Victorians, by contrast, believed they were in time to
save from extinction a workable rural economy, with its
culture intact. In the event, they were too late, but that does
not alter the fact that they held ambitious hopes for
transforming, as well as conserving the countryside by
means of practicable schemes involving the entire country
community. No such hopes or plans are tenable nowadays.
For the foreseeable future at least, ruralism, that is the belief
that an idealized way of life can be found in the country,
must content itself with contributing to the fight for
conservation, and must put aside dreams of realizing its
ideal on any scale larger than the personal and eccentric.

The reality is that all of us are to some degree alienated
from the countryside. Despite living in the 'depths' of the
country, my neighbours and I are outsiders in our own
landscape. On a national scale, the work force required to
farm the land has dwindled to the point where it is now
outnumbered by tractors, and is still declining. Less than one
per cent of Britain's population works on its agricultural
sector, which accounts for a surprising four-fifths of its
surface. The rest of us merely look on. As a result, the
countryside has been lost as much to country people, the
great majority of whom do not any more gain their
livelihood from agriculture, as to the rest of the nation. The
villager looks over his garden fence at what is happening to
the land beyond with the same feeling of separateness and
impotence as the urbanite who reads about it in his

newspaper. It was for this reason that I called my last book about the countryside *Strange Land*. We are all becoming strangers now in a land that is getting stranger every day as modern farming proceeds to strip away the features of the classic English countryside that made it so distinctive and precious.

And so, because of our dissociation from the activity that most determines the shape and appearance of our countryside, we are unavoidably strung out between memories of the past and dreams of the future, between nostalgia and utopianism. There is no middle ground in present actuality for us to occupy. Our dissociation from farming is also, to a considerable degree, responsible for our having reached the highly unsatisfactory stage of needing to rely for our contact with nature on the mediation of symbols and images, which we produce in huge quantities. The ratio of the symbolic to the actual in our relations with nature has become dangerously lopsided. But our remoteness from the country-side must be compensated for, if it cannot be mended, because it will otherwise place an insuperable obstacle in the way of our retrieving any deep-rooted sense of the significance of our lives. Indeed, I am convinced that our continuing estrangement from nature is a virtual guarantee of psycho-pathy on a national scale.

We must therefore find new ways of re-incorporating nature in our culture; or rather, we should perhaps recognize the value of those ways that already exist, but are held in contempt despite their popularity. And this brings us back to nostalgia. Our addiction to fantasies about the past is certainly a symptom of our failure to achieve a healthy mode of life in the present, but these fantasies are not to be dismissed out of hand, for they have their subversive side too. They are, after all, invariably visions of a better way of life, not a worse one. They envisage an alternative order to the accepted, established order and, to that modest degree, may be considered radical. Pastoralism itself is only an idealized image of the world in which men and women feel at home with themselves, with each other and with nature. The fact that it is conjured out of material inaccurately derived from rural history and certain persistent myths about Old England, should not detract from its worth as a dream of an improved, kindlier and more connected existence.

To sum up, I believe that a society which is addicted to nostalgic longings for a lost and largely invented countryside is probably sick, but a society which feels no longing for its countryside is sicker still.

THE COMMON OAK

Below the church and lying beside the lane that leads to
Stowlangtoft Hall is a meadow which can be crossed by
means of one of the village's few remaining footpaths.
Known as Primrose Meadow, it contains about a dozen oak
trees; many of them are venerable, while the stumps of
others, long since dead, lie in ruins beside the path. One such
stump, the remains of a tree which grew so close to its
neighbour that their branches must have locked together like
stags' antlers, has weathered to the consistency of limestone.

It is said that a free-standing tree has one inch of girth for
every year of its age, and when I measured six of the largest
trunks I found that they had an average age of 200 years.
Planting has continued since then and the most recent trees
can be dated pretty exactly to the turn of this century, since
their trunks both measure the same 82 inches. The age of the
oldest suggests they were planted in the 1760s, and it cannot
be a co-incidence that 1760 was the very year when the estate
was bought by a certain Sir Thomas Rawlinson, Bart., who
not long before had been Lord Mayor of London and M.P.
for Huntingdon. In those days Stowlangtoft's Hall stood on
a different site and the meadow would have been visible
from its windows. (That Hall was destroyed by fire and
rebuilt by the Rawlinsons in 1792, only to be pulled down
when the present, much grander Hall was erected.) In any
event, these magnificent trees were obviously planted for

their aesthetic value, as well as to provide shade for cattle and sheep.

The older trees are therefore only halfway through their life, for an age of 400 years turns out to be not at all uncommon among parkland oaks. Indeed, there is an ancient, ruined giant standing in Ickworth Park, the grounds of our nearest stately home, whose exposed rings imply an age of 700 years. The oaks in our meadow show terrible scars of dismemberment; they have all lost at least one of their huge lower limbs, which have left behind deep jagged lacerations, ripping right into the heartwood. One tree, which overshadows the road, has lost a branch that was so enormous that its collapse gouged a hole like a well out of the trunk's centre. My children climbed into this hole and it proved wide and deep enough to seat them comfortably, while completely hiding them. Another tree, growing directly in the line of the footpath, has been shattered by the loss of an even bulkier major limb. Just above my head its 20-foot trunk separates into four great branches, each as big in girth as the trunks of the younger, 80-year-old trees. Some time ago, a fifth branch grew there, stretching out westwards to the church, but when it was torn off a vast ragged cavity was wrenched out of the tree's torso. All that remains now is an outsize horse-collar of dried-up bark and sapwood. These dilapidated boughs seem to become so gross and ungainly they outgrow their strength to support themselves, and then all it takes to bring them down is a heavy fall of snow or an autumn gale. But, despite the dreadful lesions they inflict as they split off, the broken branches do not impair the tree's health; on the contrary, their loss seems to give the tree a chance to retrench its strength in middle age. On the other side of the estate, not far from our house, we can see a hedgerow oak, *all* of whose branches have long since fallen off, leaving nothing except a stump of trunk, but this

decapitated column still thrives and throws up a green nimbus of short twigs every spring.

To stand immediately beneath one of these maimed colossi is to be overwhelmed by its powerful, resonant presence. At first, I cannot help but think of it as a sailing ship, an unwieldy galleon, with its billowing sails of foliage, its creaking spars, its intricate rigging of twigs and its slow, straining action as the wind catches its topgallant branches. It reminds me of a ship too because the whole swaying canopy above narrows down to the single support of its mast-like trunk, while its roots in the earth are as invisible as a ship's keel below the water.

But then any other large, spreading tree, a beech, for instance, or a chestnut, might remind you of a sailing ship. What makes an oak so distinctive is that its entire life story is rendered legible by its contortions of growth. A beech tree, you might say, has been designed and put together according to classical principles, for its trunk is straight, tall and well buttressed, its bark is uniformly smooth, its foliage is rich and evenly spread and its shape, though generously rounded, is orderly and elegant. You can stare up into its heights and see nothing but the regular fanning out of beautifully tapering branches and drooping twigs. The narrative of its growth cannot be discerned; it has matured by a process of steady, symmetrical burgeoning as each spring deposits a fresh layer of perfection, leaving no trace of mishap or shortfall. Ironically, it is the very immaculateness of the beech's trunk that makes it the ideal medium for marking human experience: dates and initials carved in its bark keep their sharpness of outline for decades. The beech denies time by yielding nothing to age. The oak, on the other hand, is all history. Scarred, pockmarked, carbuncled, crooked, broken and invincible, an oak is the living tissue of time.

In contrast with the beech's classicism, the oak is

fashioned on Gothic lines, for it certainly exhibits an uncommon wealth of diversity in its form. Now I am struck by another image: the tree is a building whose owner cannot leave it alone, but is forever adding new wings and knocking down old ones, tinkering and adapting, renovating and redecorating. This is an owner too who is not above making mistakes and changing his mind; nor is he ashamed of his work, for all these stages are quite undigsuised. Leaning against my horse-collar oak and peering into its crazy spirals of boughs and branches, I can see here the beginnings of a massive limb, which after a few feet suddenly loses its leaves and withers into nothing; above it I can see another branch, a shrivelled, dwarfish skewer, which is nonetheless bowed down with the weight of its shimmering foliage. Here is an unexpected stretch of straight branch, its ribbed bark combed into a lovely flowing pattern, which, with a savage twist, breaks its own neck, scatters the pattern and hangs its head in a tangle of wasted twiglets. Right above me, set in the thickest part of the trunk, is an acned patch of burrs, each one sporting a tuft of green whiskers; and it is in fact these whelks and buboes that hold the juice of life, throwing out new shoots when the main branches fail.

Inevitably, I am reminded of our church, and not only because so much of it is constructed and furnished from oak. Both structures have similar histories of alteration and loss accumulating over long passages of time; both are conspicuously aged too, with their cracks and fractures, their damp and rot, their broken and rebuilt parts, and their common patina of weathering and lichen. Both possess the same rugged, ungainly hugeness, ornamented by touches of great delicacy. For example, the nicety of the flintwork set in the church porch belies the enormity of its tower, while the measured whorls coiling round the bark of the oak's trunk contradict the chaos of branches above. Only the oaks and the church are older than their landscape.

In its way, the oak is no less an institution than the church. Since our two native British oaks are not only the longest established trees in our countryside, but also dominate most of our deciduous woodlands and account for perhaps a quarter of our high forest trees, it is hardly surprising that they have become the object of adaptation for an extraordinary variety of creatures. Though no mammal is wholly reliant on the oak, most woodland species feed off it when they get the chance. Rabbits, brown hares and deer all browse oak seedlings in summer and eat acorns in winter; during very hard winter weather, rabbits eat oak bark as well. The carnivorous badger regularly eats acorns in autumn to fatten up for its hibernation. Climbing up the tree, but seldom higher than the shrub level branches, mice and voles eat acorns, together with bark, twigs, buds and any pupating insects they can find. The fat dormouse, however, prefers the loftier heights of the canopy and often makes its nest in the middle of a mature tree's crown. Here they are in competition with the grey squirrel which, unlike its rare red cousin, has a distinct preference for deciduous woodland and feeds on oak buds and acorns, burying them avidly in autumn. Tree creepers find their food on the trunk by lifting up loose scales of bark and picking off the insects below. Tits, starlings, sparrows and flycatchers put rot holes to their own use and take over any holes made by woodpeckers, which tend to occupy them for a single season only. Dozens of species of bird breed in woodland oaks, including the heron, which builds its massive, clumsy nest in the canopies of strong timber trees. In winter, these big trees are turned into overnight slums by roosting pigeons gathered together in their hundreds. Thus, an oak, especially a mature timber standard (an uncoppiced tree) carrying some dead and decaying wood, provides the services of home, hotel, summer and winter resort, tenement, storehouse, larder, refuse dump and builder's yard for its innumerable occupants and visitors. And all these vertebrates are nothing compared with the teeming invertebrate population that lives off a mature oak – 35 separate species of gall wasp alone – and turns it into an insect megalopolis.

Because of its genetic disposition to extreme variety, oaks tend to become very individualized in shape and even in the cycle of their growth: some lose their leaves in October, while others do so as late as January, and others still glow red hot in August under a second shooting of bright scarlet foliage. Whereas sycamores are difficult to tell apart, each oak is unmistakeable. No other tree displays the story of its life so conspicuously; the oak, like the human species, is highly autobiographical. Like us, the oak breaks under strain, but does not give up. Sometimes it mends itself and grows stronger than before; sometimes it abandons the struggle, but takes it up elsewhere; sometimes it succeeds magnificently, only to fail next year. It attains a battered old age, its decrepitude becoming quite visible, yet it hangs on to longevity with stubborn resistance. Just as we must build our relationships, our homes, careers, the lives of our children and a place for our dotage, so the oak too seems to have to build its trunk and branches. There is nothing smooth or spontaneous about its growth, in contrast with, say, the faultless fastigiate (broom-shaped) regularity of the Lombardy poplar; each stage of the oak's maturation appears to be the hard-won product of effort, with the result that every feature achieves a rare singularity.

Now here, to my mind, is a prime reason for conservation, and one which has not been sufficiently discussed. For the most part, conservation has concerned itself with the twin priorities of maintaining variety and protecting landscape. It has made ecological integrity its first principle and this is entirely correct, for the scale and intricacy of interdependence between species in ecologies has only recently been fully understood and is only just beginning to be taught. While this principle cannot be too heavily emphasized, there remains another need, specific to our species-being, which is not so easily satisfied by means of ordinary, broad front conservation. I mean our need, which I believe to be indispensable, for parochial monuments, landmarks, mile-stones and other points of reference by which each person can take his or her own bearings in time and place. This forms part of our ecological requirement and if it is not met we will not flourish to the height of our potential. The spirit of ecology, to be true to itself, must be extended to us, the most problematic species, and applied culturally as much as biologically. Since we are the dominant species, it would be folly to neglect us. Whereas most species tend to weaken or die out when their needs are not answered, we instead become lethally destructive – of ourselves and our world.

Like all other organisms, we demand a most delicate and penetrating relationship with our physical world, our environment, and we suffer badly when it is not adequately served. But, unlike any other organism, we are also historical beings, and we require just as complex a relationship with time. We can feel alienated from time no less acutely than from society or a hostile place. I have tried to describe the way our village is rooted in both its history and its landscape by tracing the connections that bind the church and its iconography with its raw materials, oak and flint, and by showing how they all remain properties of something that is more an idea than a place – the parish. Through these materials and the cultural nexus they form, the continuities of time and place are made visible, immediate and, above all, tangible. The flow of human experience is made meaningful. The horse-collar oak, which I have made part of my private symbolism, stands in the middle of the footpath and is therefore as much a piece of common property as the church. It may be enclosed by private land, but both its physical self and its historical presence are accessible to anyone who wishes to walk across the meadow. A living relic of Stowlangtoft's eighteenth century is there to be admired, studied, drawn or climbed. For that matter, it can be ignored too, but the point is that it endures.

The ordinary places and things that make up our everyday landscape, our personal countryside, stand as monuments to our own endurance in a way that the grand prospect never can. Without such monuments, and they are by no means a rural monopoly, our sense of identity begins to crumble and warp. We need little, low, unsuspected corners to carry special resonances for us alone. The plants and creatures that populate our local landscape give significance to our lives simply by changing and surviving beside us. They mark the narrative of our experience, while always baring the intimacy of their own: that was the spring a wren built its little sock of a nest in our woodshed only to be killed by a farm cat before its eggs hatched; that was the storm that brought down an elm across our lane; that was the summer bees swarmed in a mattress we had put out for the dustmen. Nature ages with us, and yet is constantly reborn; it is killed and rots at our feet, but springs up next year more vigorously than ever. This intermingling of our experience and its reflection in nature provides for that balanced mixture of time and place which is the ideal medium for the growth of our roots and the full flowering of our potential. By conserving the mass of precious detail in our parishes, we conserve ourselves.

In a recent essay, the American writer, Elizabeth Hardwick, tried to explain the violence of the old against the young. She wrote,

An old and enfeebled, poverty-worn person is, apparently, to the battered children of the slums an object that is contemptible and finally not quite real, for to imagine old age one has to imagine life as a long flow, something protracted by nature, and therefore meaningful in its orderly progress from one stage to another.

I think this has a profound relevance to conservation. She is of course referring to conditions in American cities, but we would be complacent to imagine that they are very different from conditions in our own cities. If its local paper is to be believed, Hackney has recently suffered from an epidemic of 'granny-rape', surely one of the most perverted and least comprehensible of all crimes against the person? But it is not only urban decadence that keeps us from being aware of the essentially organic nature of our existence, or the long flow of life, as Elizabeth Hardwick calls it. To a lesser extent, and with perhaps less grotesque consequences, country people are also becoming blind to the fact that everybody has his or her own special history, whose long unfolding needs to be respected.

Powerful forces, both cultural and economic, are battering at our subjectivity, by which I mean our sense of self, our idea of our own emotional and creative scope. An ever-encroaching uniformity is blurring the distinctiveness of time and place. Work, when it can be found, gives the majority no chance of using either imagination or initiative. Meanwhile, technological change now takes place in defiance of social need, leaving most of us in the role of helpless bystanders, or at best passive consumers of its recreational spin-offs. And, most damaging of all, our ethical life has been reduced to a chaos of pragmatic convenience: morality is seen as a restrictive, punitive force, an outmoded constraint to be shrugged off wherever it binds, and its capacity to unite people under a shared recognition of common purpose has been forgotten. We are in danger of living in an eternal present, dissociated from tradition and devoid of aspiration for the future: without memory or hope.

Our loss of familiarity with nature is only one of the constrictions on our humanity, and it has to be admitted that a successful conservation programme, in itself, would not usher in a new, liberated phase of history. On the other hand, a renewal of our relationship with nature, which on a limited basis is within the reach of our present institutions, would be inseparable from a greatly sharpened awareness, if nothing else, of the other forces belittling our capacity for self-realization. A closer intimacy with nature would bring us an understanding of that 'orderly progress from one stage to another' that Elizabeth Hardwick wrote about. But intimacy of this order is not possible on a theoretical level; it is more than a question of education and the provision of facilities, for it can only be achieved by a continuing, day-by-day involvement with particular plants, creatures or corners of nature. Hence the crucial need for the small-scale conservation, in towns no less than the countryside, of local landscapes, which may not be spectacular, nor endowed with rarities, but which are rich in associations for the people living beside them.

Binsey Poplars
felled 1879

My aspens dear, whose airy cages quelled,
Quelled or quenched in leaves the leaping sun,
All felled, felled, are all felled;
  Of a fresh and following folded rank
        Not spared, not one
        That dandled a sandalled
      Shadow that swam or sank
On meadow and river and wind-wandering weed-winding
  bank.

  O if we but knew what we do
      When we delve or hew –
    Hack and rack the growing green!
      Since country is so tender
    To touch, her being só slender,
    That, like this sleek and seeing ball
    But a prick will make no eye at all,
    Where we, even where we mean
        To mend her we end her,
      When we hew or delve:
After-comers cannot guess the beauty been.
    Ten or twelve, only ten or twelve
      Strokes of havoc únselve
        The sweet especial scene,
      Rural scene, a rural scene,
      Sweet especial rural scene.

Gerard Manley Hopkins, 1879

NOTES

Introduction

1. *Nature Conservancy in Great Britain*, Nature Conservancy Council, 1984, p. 50.

Our Conker Tree

1. Jay Appleton, *The Experience of Landscape*, London: John Wiley & Sons, 1975, p. 67.
2. Erich Isaac, 'Myths, Cults and Livestock Breeding', *Diogenes*, Spring, 1963, p. 75.

Wild Flowers

1. Keith Thomas, *Man and the Natural World*, London: Allen Lane, 1983, p. 18.
2. John Ruskin, *Modern Painters*, George Routledge, 1843–1860 Vol V, X, §7.

Village Gothic

1. Stephen Jay Gould, *The Panda's Thumb*, London: Penguin, 1980, p. 11.

Birds

1. Richard Mabey, *The Common Ground*, London: Hutchinson, 1980, p. 194.

NOTES

2. Claude Lévi-Strauss, *The Savage Mind*, London: Weidenfeld & Nicolson, 1972, p. 204.
3. I am indebted throughout this passage to E. S. Turner, *All Heaven in a Rage*, London: Michael Joseph 1964.
4. Ed. Peggy Munsterberg, *The Penguin Book of Bird Poetry*, London: Penguin 1984, p. 98.

The Genius of Childhood

1. Ronald Blythe, *From the Headlands*, London: Chatto & Windus, 1982, p. 4.

Positive Nostalgia

1. Willis H. McCann, 'Nostalgia: A Rearview of the Literature', *Psychological Bulletin*, Vol. 38, No. 3, March 1941, p. 196.
2. Jan Marsh, *Back to the Land*, Quartet Books, 1982, p. 7.

Common Oak

1. Elizabeth Hardwick, *Barnaby in Manhattan & Other Essays*, Weidenfeld & Nicolson, 1983.